General editor: Graham Handley MA Ph.D.

Brodie's Notes on Arthur Miller's

Death of a Salesman

J. B. E. Turner MA

M
MACMILLAN

First published by James Brodie Ltd
This revised edition first published 1990
by Pan Books Ltd

Reprinted 1992 by
THE MACMILLAN PRESS LTD
Houndmills, Basingstoke, Hampshire RG21 2XS
and London
Companies and representatives
throughout the world

ISBN 0-333-58153-9

Printed in Great Britain by
Clays Ltd, St Ives plc, Bungay, Suffolk

These notes are based on the Penguin edition of *Death of a
Salesman*, but, as reference is made throughout to each of the
two Acts and their eposides, and the Requiem at the end, the
Notes can be used with any edition of the printed play.

Contents

Preface

The intention throughout this study aid is to stimulate and guide, to encourage your involvement in the book, and to develop informed responses and a sure understanding of the main details.

Brodie's Notes provide a clear outline of the play or novel's plot, followed by act, scene, or chapter summaries and/or commentaries. These are designed to emphasize the most important literary and factual details. Poems, stories or non-fiction texts combine brief summary with critical commentary on individual aspects or common features of the genre being examined. Textual notes define what is difficult or obscure and emphasize literary qualities. Revision questions are set at appropriate points to test your ability to appreciate the prescribed book and to write accurately and relevantly about it.

In addition, each of these Notes includes a critical appreciation of the author's art. This covers such major elements as characterization, style, structure, setting and themes. Poems are examined technically – rhyme, rhythm, for instance. In fact, any important aspect of the prescribed work will be evaluated. The aim is to send you back to the text you are studying.

Each study aid concludes with a series of general questions which require a detailed knowledge of the book: some of these questions may invite comparison with other books, some will be suitable for coursework exercises, and some could be adapted to work you are doing on another book or books. Each study aid has been adapted to meet the needs of the current examination requirements. They provide a basic, individual and imaginative response to the work being studied, and it is hoped that they will stimulate you to acquire disciplined reading habits and critical fluency.

Graham Handley 1990

The author and his work

Arthur Miller was born in the Harlem district of New York City in 1915, of middle-class Jewish parents; his father was a manufacturer of ladies' coats, his mother a former teacher. In 1928 the family moved to Brooklyn, which in those days, in its rural nature, resembled the Lomans' environment before it was stifled by buildings. Like Biff Loman, Miller was a keen footballer; he did not shine at his studies, however, was rejected by two universities and went to work in his father's garment factory. It was here, after getting to know the buyers and salesmen, that he became unhappy about human relationships in industry and wrote his first story, an angry study of an ageing salesman – the seed that was to grow into *Death of a Salesman*.

Miller left the garment factory after only a few months and tried various jobs. He was by now reading a great deal of good literature, no doubt as compensation for the lack of satisfaction he found in industry. This obviously stood him in good stead, for, when he decided to re-apply for university, he was accepted by Michigan. He thoroughly enjoyed his life there, reading English and studying journalism, with a part-time job as night-editor of the *Michigan Daily*. He also began writing plays, and won an award for *Honors at Dawn* (1936), which reflected the economic depression America was suffering at the time, and which attacked the social system. The following year another play, *No Villain*, was produced and, in its revised edition, re-named *They Too Arise*, won an award. The interesting feature for our study is that both plays introduce family conflicts, and *They Too Arise* depicts a father who suffers, like Willy Loman, from an illusion which he tries to impose on his sons.

In 1938 Miller graduated, and two years later married Mary Slattery. He took a number of jobs, including truck-driving and steam-fitting in the Navy Yard, while all the time writing for radio. An old football injury kept him out of the army, but he came into close contact with the troops in army camps when he was gathering material for a film, *The Story of GI Joe*, and a book, *Situation Normal* (1944). In 1945 a novel, *Focus*, was published. Meanwhile he was working on *All My Sons*, which was to be the first of his well-known plays. It took him two years to write, and when produced in 1947, it won the New York Drama Critics' Circle Award. The play deals in part with the conflict between the family and society, and a son's admiration for his father receives a shattering setback. Critics consider that the influence of the great Norwegian dramatist, Ibsen, whom Miller had studied, is noticeable in the careful structure, the relationship between past and present, the themes of the sins of the parents being visited on the children and of a life being built on a lie – all facets which we shall discover in *Death of a Salesman*.

In 1949 *Death of a Salesman* was first produced and was received with unanimous enthusiasm by the critics, winning six prizes and awards. It was written in six weeks, but, as we have seen, the idea was born years before. The film version followed in 1951, and a television production in 1966.

In 1950 Miller's adaptation of Ibsen's play, *An Enemy of the People*, was produced, followed in 1953 by *The Crucible*, which was a parable of the hysterical, anti-communist, McCarthy witch hunts that were taking place in America. 1955 saw the premières of two more plays: *A Memory of Two Mondays* and *A View From the Bridge*.

These were hectic years for Miller, beginning in the spring of 1955, when he accepted an offer to write a filmscript about the New York City Youth Board's work with juvenile gangs. The presentation of his script coincided with a strong attack in the *New York World-Telegram*, charging him with left-wing activities, and the House Un-American Activities Committee backed up the newspaper's demand that New York City should cancel their agreement with him. The Mayor of New York called for a report on Miller's background but nothing more subversive was discovered than that, in his youth, Miller had been attracted to Marxism, had attended several meetings of Communist writers in 1947 and, when the party was outlawed, had signed a protest. The Mayor then declared that no evidence of left-wing association had been found, and thought the City should go ahead with his script for the film. Unfortunately for Miller, the City's Board of Estimate had to approve the contract, which was promptly opposed by three powerful members of the Board. Miller was asked to make a public apology for his past left-wing relationship; angrily, he refused. Opposition grew, and when in 1956 he applied for a passport to visit England to arrange the production of *A View from the Bridge*, he was ordered to appear before the House Un-American Activities Committee.

Before the committee, Miller defended not so much Communism as an author's right to be totally involved in the social commitments of his time, and to be allowed the free expression of his opinions. The committee reminded him of his past defence of Communist activities and of his satirical attack (in *The Nation*, 1954) on the investigating committee itself.. The climax of his appearance before the committee came when they demanded to know the names of the other writers present at the meetings in 1947, threatening to cite him with contempt of Congress if he refused to divulge the information. Miller stated that he would be willing to answer questions about himself but that under no circumstances would he involve others. The meeting was adjourned for ten days, and Miller wrote to the Chairman:

I know myself to be a person devoted to democratic institutions and opposed to totalitarianism. The meetings in question occurred nearly ten years ago. At that time, the Communist Party, as far as I was aware, had not been declared a conspiracy, but was legally recognized and accorded the privilege of a political party ... On the ground of their participating in illegal actions, therefore, I cannot justify myself in naming these people ... (Quoted in the *New York Times*, 11 July 1956).

Despite this, Miller was prosecuted and convicted for contempt of Congress. He was fined five hundred dollars and given a suspended prison sentence of one month. But 1958 brought victory – he won a complete reversal of the verdict in the Court of Appeals.

Miller had been divorced from his first wife in 1956, and shortly afterwards married Marilyn Monroe, one of the most famous film stars of her time. For the next few years it was *her* career that flourished; and Miller, acting as her unofficial manager, allowed his own to lie dormant. The marriage gradually deteriorated, and in 1961 they were divorced. In that year Miller's film, *The Misfits*, was produced.

1964 saw the production of Miller's first play for nearly nine years – *After the Fall*, in which the leading character analyses his part in his two failed marriages. This was followed by *Incident at Vichy* (1965), *I Don't Need You Any More* (a collection of short stories, 1967), *The Price* (1968), *In Russia* (1969), *The Creation of the World and Other Business* (1972) and a musical play, *Up from Paradise* (1974).

(*Note:* We have endeavoured here to give the correct date of, in each case, the first performance of a play or showing of a film. But this is a notoriously difficult task, due, we believe, to the tendency of some authorities to give the date when the author finished writing the *script*. Thus, the various encyclopedias and biographical dictionaries seem unable to agree with one another about dates.)

Plot

Willy Loman, sixty-three years old and a travelling salesman for a New York City firm for thirty-six years, is in the last stages of exhaustion and heading for suicide. He returns home to New York with his sales mission to New England unattempted, because he could not prevent his car from running off the road. His wife, Linda, tries as always to comfort him. His sons, Biff and Happy, are paying one of their rare visits home and we see at once that Biff and his father are at loggerheads. In a series of flashbacks we see that this friction was not always there, but we also see its cause.

Willy hero-worships Biff and is immensely proud of his good looks, athletic ability and attractive personality. He brings his sons up to follow the shallow philosophy that these are the only things that count in life. Willy not only believes that to be well liked is all that matters, but also clings blindly to the mistaken belief that he is himself a successful salesman because he is well-liked. We learn just how false is his dream when Linda tells her sons that Willy often sells nothing, that his fixed salary has been stopped, and that he borrows money from his neighbour every week, pretending it is his pay.

A later flashback (Biff, having failed his examination to qualify for university, pays a surprise visit to his father in Boston – to enlist his help in persuading his tutor to alter the examination result) shows the critical moment when disillusion destroys the mutual admiration of father and son: Biff discovers his father with a mistress. Horror struck, he abandons all idea of university and tries to find escape in a variety of jobs, prospering at none and losing most of them through petty theft. Willy reacts by suspecting Biff is always trying to spite him, and his constant criticism of Biff is inspired mainly by his own sense of guilt.

Happy, the younger brother, was never the favourite that Biff was and his pathetic attempts to seek attention are ignored by his father. He goes into business and, though less restless than Biff, is not really satisfied by his job and his hobby of womanizing.

Uncle Charley and his son Bernard are neighbours. They are a contrast to the Lomans, Charley being a quiet, efficient and successful owner of a business. Bernard, who irritatingly points out Biff's avoidance of work at High School and then announces the examination failure, grows into a mature and successful young lawyer. Charley is kind to Willy and repeatedly offers him a job in his own firm; Willy, jealous at heart, responds as if he had been insulted.

Uncle Ben, Willy's elder brother, who appears only in Willy's imagination, is used to illustrate the dormant pioneer in Willy. (Their father crossed the States by wagon, selling home-made flutes. Willy, when a young man, was tempted to go adventuring – like brother Ben, who is reputed to have made a fortune in diamonds.) He thinks, with frustration, about the glamour of such a life compared with his routine existence. And the thrill of wide open spaces, or of jungles, contrasts with the stifling nature of the overbuilt and overpopulated city. Uncle Ben is held up to Biff and Happy as someone to be admired and he, in turn, is asked to admire the 'rugged spirit' of the boys exemplified in their pilfering from a building site – moral values are of secondary importance.

Towards the end of the first act Linda makes it plain to her sons that their help and support should have been a good deal more freely given. Their father is in a pitiable predicament: his car accidents are suspected to have been deliberate and she has discovered a piece of tubing and a new connection on the gas pipe in the cellar.

This is not, however, the real climax: the tension eases at the end of the act. The brothers are exploring the possibility of starting a business together – 'The Loman Brothers'. Biff will seek his first employer's sponsorship the following day, and Willy will ask his boss for an office job. They all go to bed excited at what they believe to be a turn of the tide in their affairs.

The second act begins in the same optimistic vein. The sons are to stand their father a dinner in town as a celebration. Willy arrives at Howard's (his employer's) office, keyed up to ask for an office job, but has to listen to Howard's tape-recording of his family. When he is at last able to make his request, explaining that he would rather not travel any more, Howard replies that there is no other job available. Willy pathetically begs for an office job, saying he would accept fifty dollars a week; Howard responds by firing him.

Alone and exhausted, Willy's mind returns to the past and to

Ben's offer of an exciting job in Alaska. Linda, playing for security, persuades him to refuse. The boys come in and Willy, showing off in front of Ben, boasts of Biff's success, which he attributes to his being 'well-liked'. When Ben goes, the family leave for the ball-game in which Biff is to shine.

Returning to present time, we see Willy in Charley's office, where he has gone to borrow more money. He meets Bernard, now a successful lawyer, and thinks sadly of his own sons; desperately, he asks Bernard to tell him the secret of his success. Bernard, however, probes Willy's mind about Biff's sudden change of direction after the visit to Boston; Willy, on the defensive, angrily avoids the answer. Charley arrives and, in reply to Willy's request for yet another loan, again offers him a job with his firm but Willy's pride will not permit him to accept. Charley then gives Willy the money.

The restaurant scene which follows is far from the celebration it was intended to be. Before Willy arrives, Happy has flirted with a call-girl and asked her to find a 'friend' for Biff. Willy is eager to hear how Biff has fared in his attempt to persuade Oliver to sponsor him – but Biff has had no more success than Willy. He waited hours for an interview with Oliver, approached him as he was leaving, but was not recognized. He reacted by stealing Oliver's fountain pen. The double shock is too much for Willy; he is left 'babbling in the toilet', while Biff rushes off into the city and Happy follows with the two girls.

There follows the critical scene in Boston (in the past), when Biff, after failing his examination, seeks help from his father; but discovers him sharing a room with a strange woman. His illusions are shattered, his idol debased, and he surrenders to failure in life. Willy is never again relaxed in Biff's presence: but always guilty, always on the defensive, suspecting Biff of antagonizing him from spite, while at the same time longing for Biff's love.

Back home, the sons have returned to a justifiably enraged Linda, who spares no words to tell them how vilely they have treated their father. Biff is repentant. He discovers his father sowing seeds in the yard by torchlight.

Willy talks to Ben as he sows, disclosing his plan to commit suicide so that Biff can have his life insurance money and become a success, and respect and love his father again. Biff tries to calm Willy and takes the blame for their estrangement.

But Willy will not shake hands with his son nor will he face the truth that they are both failures. Eventually Biff breaks down, sobbing and clutching his father. Willy, ecstatically, realizes that Biff still loves him.

There is, however, no happy ending. The sudden enlightenment only increases Willy's determination to endow Biff with the means for success by his own death. He waits until the others have gone upstairs, drives off in the car and is killed.

The 'Requiem' amplifies the tragedy. Charley blames Willy's job for his death. Happy, still deluded, believes Willy was right to live his dream. Poor Linda is bewildered that Willy should have done this just as they were out of debt. Biff alone has found the truth about himself and his father: 'He had the wrong dreams. All, all, wrong . . . He never knew who he was.'

Themes

1 Willy's 'Wrong Dreams'

Arthur Miller is considered by many to be one of the most important living dramatists; *Death of a Salesman* is one of his greatest plays. In all his works, he says, his concern is 'with the aspirations, worries and failures of all men – and more especially of the little man . . .' Miller's intention in displaying their aspirations, worries and failures is both to entertain and to heighten the awareness of his audience to the nature of modern life and in *Death of a Salesman* he wanted to 'set forth what happens when a man does not have a grip on the forces of life and has no sense of values which will lead him to that kind of grip'. 'The play,' said Miller, 'was begun with only one firm piece of knowledge, and this was that Loman was to destroy himself.' These two statements, which constitute the main theme of the play, are related: Willy has lost touch with life and is heading for self-destruction. He has set his sights on 'success'. His idols are Dave Singleman, an 84-year-old salesman whose strong personality had commanded success, and Ben, his elder brother, who had found wealth colourfully, romantically, by walking into the jungle and discovering diamonds. To Willy therefore, success means two things – being rich and being popular. To these ends Willy strives to the point of obsession. As Miller says, '. . . his sin was to have committed himself so completely to the counterfeits of dignity and the false coinage embodied in his idea of success . . .'

By the time the play begins, Willy has failed utterly to achieve either of his goals. He is comparatively poor, he has to borrow fifty dollars a week from Charley to keep himself and Linda alive, and, in a moment of truth, he admits that far from being well liked he is a laughing stock. Nevertheless, his obsession is rampant; he *will* keep up the pretence of success at all costs, he *will* live a lie. He is a 'vital salesman' – 'I did five hundred gross in Providence and seven hundred gross in Boston.' His will be an equally great success – '. . . three great universities are begging for him'. 'A man can end up with diamonds here on the basis of being liked!' 'I am not a dime a dozen! I am Willy Loman.'

The main theme, then, is Willy's 'wrong dreams', and his conscious attempt to pretend to himself and others that he was not failing to realize them. This pretence is essential to Willy:

Willy Loman has broken a law without whose protection life is insupportable if not incomprehensible to him and to many others; it is the law which says that a failure in society has no right to live.

A harsh law, to be mitigated in the secondary theme – the relationship between Willy and Biff:

My attempt in the play was to counter this anxiety with an opposing system which, so to speak, is in a race for Willy's faith, and it is the system of love which is the opposite of the law of success. It is embodied in Biff Loman . . .

2 Willy and Biff

The relationship between father and son in the 'past time' of the play shows both strength and weakness. Willy worships his son's athletic prowess, his good looks and his popularity; Biff, in turn, idolizes his father. He is prepared to score at the ball-game especially for him. This mutual admiration is handicapped by Willy's continual indoctrination of his son with his own shallow ideas of 'success' and popularity, combined with his extravagant expectations of Biff's rapid rise to success, and it appears to break down completely when Biff discovers that his idol is being unfaithful to his mother. And so we arrive at the present time of the play. Biff is a drifter with a history of petty theft, and his father, guilty and suspicious, attributes Biff's every move to spite. Willy's obsession is now twofold: firstly, as we have seen, to live the lie of achieved success, and secondly, to regain his elder son's love and acknowledgement of his, Willy's, success.

At the end of the play the second of these obsessions seems to be satisfied. Biff breaks down, clutching his father, and Willy cries, '. . . isn't that remarkable? Biff – he likes me!' There is an echo of King Lear's '. . . look, her lips – look there, look there! . . .' But the re-emergence of love between the two is not to be the catharsis of the play. It is too late. Willy, still blinded by the illusory light of financial success, kills himself to endow Biff with the means to follow that light.

The second theme is completed by Biff's discovery of the truth about himself: 'I know who I am, kid.' But Willy has died in an attempt to perpetuate the wrong dreams and is no more enlightened at the end than was Othello at *his* end calling for acclamation of himself as a heroic warrior. The counter-balance which Miller intended is not entirely successful – Biff's revelation does not atone for his father's obduracy.

The nature of the play

1 The Social System

The play, then, is about Willy's predicament and what caused it. Was it the fault of society, of capitalism, of a system that grinds its weaker brethren to destruction? Was it Willy's fault for dreaming the wrong dreams? Is the play a tragedy, or a social drama with a strong note of propaganda and a flavour of compassion? Some ask 'Does it really matter which it is?' The answer is, it does, because those who ask the question use the term 'tragedy' as a 'value word'. If it is a tragedy then it is a 'good' play, if it is just a social drama then it is not so 'good'! Miller's own writings are very helpful in trying to solve this question. First, on the play as a sociological drama:

I am not calling for ideology, I am simply asking for a theater in which an adult who wants to live can find plays that will heighten his awareness of what living in our time involves.

Then, defending the author's right to relate his plays to their time, he wrote:

Society is inside of man and man is inside of society, and you cannot even create a truthfully drawn psychological entity on the stage until you understand his social relations and their power to make him what he is and prevent him from being what he is not. The fish is in the water, and the water is in the fish.

Miller is a social dramatist in the broad sense of the word. He was greatly affected by the depression that sickened America in the late nineteen-twenties and, not unnaturally, the symptoms of the disease are portrayed in his dramas. In *Death of a Salesman* the greatest indictment of the ruling social system is that it insists on an image of 'success' in which money and power are everything. Willy accepts this image and blindly and obsessively makes it his goal. He tries to close his eyes to his wretched failure, only to realize a final solution in death.

There are other, more particular, criticisms of the social system in the play. Willy is discarded when he becomes exhausted after serving his company for nearly thirty-six years. He has spent his life trying to earn enough money to pay instalments on articles which have become necessities in the twentieth century but which wear out before they are paid for. This life of frustration has for its setting an overcrowded environment where nothing natural will grow.

A number of critics, prejudiced, no doubt, by Arthur Miller's own attraction to Marxism in his early days, and his defence of various communist activities, assert that the play is communist propaganda, and that Willy is destroyed by the capitalist system. This assertion is not difficult to refute; if it *is* true, why did Miller make Charley and Bernard, members of the same class as Willy, live successfully within the system? Charley is even a capitalist employer and his treatment in the play is wholly sympathetic – Miller obviously approves of him. Even more significant, however, is the fact that Miller berates not only society but Willy himself, who is partly a victim of his environment but also of his own will and choice.

It is less easy to answer the criticism that the emphasis of the play is on the social forces to such an extent that Willy never achieves any degree of heroic stature. If we can refute this as well we may claim that the play is a tragedy.

2 Willy's fault?

One of the early rules for tragedy, propounded by Aristotle, was hat the hero must be of high rank so that his fall may be the reater. Many critics assert that Willy is just a little victim of his ociety, one who has consented to live society's lie and who gains ıo size from the predicament in which it places him. But Miller maintains that Aristotle's rule no longer holds and, 'So long as the hero may be said to have had alternatives of a magnitude to have materially changed the course of his life, it seems to me that, in this respect at least, he cannot be debarred from the heroic role.'

Can it, then, be shown that Willy had 'alternatives', that he was not just a victim of the ruling social system which drove him down the path to destruction, but that he had a choice of paths, one of which might have saved him? To have acknowledged such a choice he had to be aware of his predicament; we have only to look at the moments of truth he faces to realize that he knew he was wrong in pretending to be successful and living a lie. Had he accepted the choice of honestly admitting he would never be rich and popular, swallowing his pride and taking a job with Charley's firm, he would then, as Miller remarks, '. . . have died contentedly while polishing his car, probably on a Sunday afternoon with the ball-game coming over the radio.' And how disappointed we should be! For all his 'wrong dreams', Willy is a hero: he knows he has an alternative, but he has set his sights on success and is prepared to die for it. And Willy does live and die for his dream.

Finally, Miller contends that the problems the hero faces must be of a universal nature, the kind that affect us all: '. . . the questions, in short, whose answers define humanity and the right way to live so that the world is a home, instead of a battleground'.

To the ancient Greeks such problems were about man's relationship with the gods. In modern times they concern man's relationship to society; and Miller claims that the play fulfils this condition by dealing with 'social laws of action no less powerful in their effect upon individuals than any tribal law administered by gods with names'. Willy's great battle is with these laws in trying to secure what he considers to be his just rights. 'The tragic feeling is evoked in us,' Miller says, 'when we are in the presence of a character who is ready to lay down his life, if need be, to secure one thing – his personal dignity . . . to gain his "rightful" position in his society.' Willy is certainly such a character.

Structure and setting

Structure

The first problem the play presents is the time factor; episodes alternate between what in this Study Aid is called 'present time' and 'past time'. Miller intended to create a form of drama which would literally be the process of Willy Loman's mind, and he achieved this by adopting the 'stream of consciousness' technique. In *Death of a Salesman* this is both suitable and effective, since Willy's exhausted mind naturally re-lives many of the episodes of his past which have gone to shape his present.

Film directors frequently switch to the past to explain the present, which many years ago came to be known as the 'flashback' method; in this Study Aid, for the sake of brevity, past scenes are sometimes referred to as 'flashbacks'. Miller, however, stresses that there are no flashbacks in the cinematic sense in this play: '... only a mobile concurrence of past and present' as it actually exists in Willy's mind.

The past episodes are cleverly introduced by a link with the present-time episodes which . precede them, with the 'past' dialogue intricately interwoven with the 'present'. Most important, one recognizes that the information they provide about Willy's past is the essential complement to his present, and that only the combination of the two enables us to see 'The Inside of his Head' which was, in fact, the original title of this play.

Setting

The difficulties to be overcome in staging this play are not immediately obvious; they stem mainly from the time sequences discussed in the last section. There are at least twenty changes of scene, and in some the action is an instantaneous change from the present to the past and back again, with the same actors, playing a scene in the present, who suddenly have to appear as they were fifteen years before.

The stage directions for Act 1 give a set consisting of a skeleton house surrounded by the towering shapes of apartment houses, and fronted by a stretch of bare fore-stage referred to as the apron. There are three rooms: a kitchen at the centre; Willy and Linda's bedroom to the right and on a level two feet higher than the kitchen; and the sons' bedroom, set back from the kitchen and on a level 1.98m (6½ ft) above it.

In the present-time scenes the actors behave normally, as if it were a real house, and changes of scene from one room to another are made simply by dimming the lights on the first room and bringing them up to the second. In the past-time scenes, which occur in Willy's mind only, the actors behave abnormally, ignoring the walls of the house (or, rather, where the walls would be if it were not a skeleton house) and walking through them from one room to another, or from inside to outside.

Scenes not set in the house are staged on the apron, which becomes at different times the meeting place for Willy and Ben, Howard's office, Charley's office, Frank's Chop House, the Woman's room in Boston, and the graveyard.

The original production was staged with great ingenuity by the famous American scene designer, Jo Mielziner, who said afterwards that his biggest problem was the scene in which the two grown up sons go to bed in full view of the audience, seconds later appearing downstage as young boys dressed for football. Mielziner overcame this by having an inner frame built in the beds, with quiet 'pulley' apparatus, which lowered the boys to a point on the stage concealed from the audience by the set, from where they could slip offstage, change, and make their appearance on time.

Language and music

Language

The use of the 'stream of consciousness' method, the setting with its dream-like sequences aided by light and music, are all an oblique way of heightening our sharing of the experience of Willy's suffering – Miller is using the techniques of expressionism. The rest of the play is in stark contrast to this: it is completely naturalistic. This is evidenced by the dialogue, which, except for a very few passages, such as Linda's plea for attention for Willy, is thoroughly ordinary conversation. It abounds in the catch-phrases, slang and jargon of American, twentieth-century, urban, lower-middle-class life. A few examples are: Chevvy, aspirin, showing the line, lazy bum, simonize, ball-game, sneakers, ads, shoot a little casino, faulty fridges, life insurances, instalment payments, fired, strapped, cover girl, size nine sheers. The conversation is filled with clichés, hesitations, *non sequiturs*, and at times it is almost inarticulate. This suits the play's theme admirably, for it is itself a criticism of the emptiness of the way of life it records.

Music

Music is used to great effect; there is the flute music, 'small and fine, telling of grass and trees and the horizon', which reminds us of happier days when Willy's house was still in a rural environment. It also reminds us of Willy's pioneer father, the flute-maker/salesman, and the American dream of success in the wide open spaces. There is the gay, light music, associated with the sons when they are young, and there is Ben's idyllic music which accompanies his entries and tells of high romance in far away places. There is the raucous music to accompany the red glow which denotes the bizarre restaurant scene, the trumpet mote which accompanies Bernard's announcement of Biff's examination failure, and the raw, sensuous music to suit the Boston scene. Finally there is the music which accompanies Willy's last exit, and the sound of the car, which, if the action and dialogue were removed, would tell the end of the story by itself:

Suddenly music, faint and high, stops him. It rises in intensity, almost to an unbearable scream . . . As the car speeds off, the music crashes down in a frenzy of sound, which becomes the soft pulsation of a single 'cello string . . . The music has developed into a dead march

And to the close of the play:

Only the music of the flute is left on the darkening stage as over the house the hard towers of the apartment building rise into sharp focus.

Summaries of episodes, textual notes and revision questions

Note: The Play, as in many modern plays is not divided into numbered scenes and consists of only two Acts. It does, however, fall naturally into episodes – seven in each act and the final 'Requiem'. For the purpose of these notes, the episodes will be taken separately.

Act 1, episode 1 pp.7–14

The lengthy stage directions are important and reference should be made to our notes on pages 18–21.

It is night, Willy Loman, the salesman, returns home with his two large suitcases of samples. He is over sixty and is obviously exhausted. His wife Linda is worried at his unexpected return. She questions him gently and learns that he never reached his destination, as he kept driving the car off the road. Linda attempts to comfort him, urging him to ask to be transferred to the office in New York and give up travelling. We learn that his two sons, on a rare visit home, are asleep in the house, and that the relationship between Willy and his elder son is strained. Willy considers that Biff is a lazy waster. Linda tries to pacify Willy, who responds, and, in a quickly changed mood, remembers how proud he was of Biff as a high school student. But Willy's depression soon returns and he laments the urbanization of his once rural home. The episode closes with Willy mixing past and present haphazardly in his mind.

melody ... upon a flute (stage directions) The flute note, telling of grass and trees and the horizon, sets the atmosphere of earlier days before urbanization; it reminds us too of Willy's pioneer father, the flute seller, and of the 'American Dream'.
apartment houses Blocks of flats as opposed to Willy's little house.
dormer window Upright window set in a sloping roof.
draped Curtained.
mercurial Lively, volatile temperament.
Yonkers A district of New York City – so Willy did not get far.
Studebaker A make of car.
Florida America's famous holiday state.

arch supports Willy, suffering, no doubt, after all his walking with
heavy cases, wears inserts in his shoes to stop the curve of his instep
from flattening.

I opened the windshield Cars of the 1920s had windscreens which
swivelled open to provide a cooling draught. Willy is a little
bewildered; he thinks he was driving his old Chevrolet car of 1928.

New England The five Eastern states of: Connecticut, Massachusetts,
Rhode Island, New Hampshire and Maine.

Portland A New England coast town.

to show the line To exhibit his samples.

life is a casting off Linda's philosophy is that in ever changing life, one
thing gives way to another.

bum A tramp.

high school American equivalent of English secondary school.

Thomas Edison . . . One of them was deaf The American inventor and
pioneer industrialist of the phonograph, the incandescent light, the
moving picture camera and the developer of the telegraph and
telephone, was deaf from an early age.

B. F. Goodrich The American industrialist who began his career in
medicine, switched to real estate and finally to rubber manufacture at
which he became successful, but not until he was thirty-eight.

Chevvy Chevrolet car.

simonize the name of a car polish and here used as a verb, to polish.

Act 1, episode 2, pp.14–21

The light now illumines the sons' room – and Happy, the
younger boy by two years, is heard telling Biff of his fears for
their father's safety on the road. In the background, Willy can be
heard voicing scattered reminiscences to himself. The sons, too,
reminisce, because it is years since they visited home together.
Their memories are of the girls they have won. Happy then
introduces the theme of the friction between Willy and Biff. Biff
complains of his father's mockery. Happy replies that Willy talks
to himself – complaining to Biff, in his imagination – because
Biff will not settle down. Biff, in self-defence, asks Happy not to
blame his father's condition on him; and he hints that he knows
of something that is depressing Willy, but he will not disclose
what this is. The sons then discuss Biff's career to date. It is an
unsatisfactory attempt to escape a routine existence and it has
led to twenty or thirty jobs, mainly on farms in the West. Happy
then admits to his own restlessness. He has achieved comparat-
ive affluence but is lonely and unsatisfied.

Fired by a sudden burst of enthusiasm from Biff, the brothers discuss the possibility of running a ranch together out West. They exult in this wonderful dream of independence in the great open spaces, until Happy rudely awakens them by asking how much money you can make that way, and then admits that he wants material success first. They return to the subject of their sexual conquests, Happy boasting of seducing girls already engaged to colleagues of his. Biff now calls to mind his first employer Oliver and, though he admits he resigned from his first job rather than be fired for theft, he considers going to Oliver for a loan to start a ranch. At this juncture Willy is heard talking to himself. After Happy has asked Biff to talk to Willy in the morning, the brothers go to sleep.

There's one or two other things depressing him This is the first hint of
  Biff's 'secret', his knowledge of his father's infidelity which has such a
  great effect on his life.
Nebraska, the Dakotas, Arizona, Texas Mid-west and West States
  where farming and ranching predominated (and still do).
merchandise manager Chief buyer.
Long Island Contains the western end of New York City, and
  Brooklyn.

Act 1, episode 3, pp.21–6

The surrounding apartment houses fade out; leaves appear everywhere; we hear music telling us to follow Willy into the past. Young Biff and Happy are polishing the car while Willy watches and advises. Willy then gives them a present of a punch-bag with Gene Tunney's signature on it. Biff shows his father a new football he has 'borrowed' from school. Willy condones this theft, emphasizing that to be liked is what matters most, and then tells the boys he will have his own business one day. He boasts of his latest trip and promises to take them with him in the summer. The conversation then turns to the ball-game to be played that afternoon. Biff is captain of his school team and promises to score a touchdown especially for his father. Bernard, Charley's son, comes in. He warns 'Uncle' Willy that Biff is not working hard enough to pass his exams. Willy despises Bernard, calling him an anaemic, and tells his own boys that Bernard may do well academically but that they, with their good looks and personalities, will soon outstrip him in the business world. He boasts of his own popularity and success as a salesman.

chamois Leather used for polishing.
Gene Tunney The heavyweight World Champion boxer in the
  nineteen-twenties.
I'm losing weight, you notice, Pop? Happy tries too hard for
  attention.
Providence, Waterbury, Boston, Portland, Bangor Important towns
  in the New England states. Boston, the cradle of the revolution,
  because the 'Boston Tea-party' marked the start of the Colonists'
  defiance of the mother country.
Mass. Massachusetts.
game The American ball-game which resembles British rugby football.
Regents A public examination, taken in various different subjects at
  the end of each High-School year, to qualify for university entrance.
flunk Fail.
sneakers Gym shoes (black), or tennis shoes (white).
Adonises Adonis, in Greek mythology, was a youth loved by Venus for
  his beauty.

Act 1, episode 4, pp.26–31

Linda enters, as of old, and Biff and Happy leave to join their
friends and hang up the washing for her. Linda asks Willy what
he sold on his last trip and Willy tells of twelve hundred gross,
which is quickly reduced to two hundred gross when Linda
starts reckoning his commission. The true reckoning, given by
Linda, shows that his commission nowhere near covers his hire-
purchase and other debts for the month. Willy's former mood of
deluded optimism now changes into one of self-pitying pess-
imism. He is a failure; he is fat and buyers laugh at him or
ignore him; maybe he talks too much. Linda denies all his
self-accusations and encourages him in his former optimistic
illusions. Willy begins to praise Linda gratefully, but a woman's
laughter is heard from the darkness and then she is dimly seen,
dressing. Willy continues to talk of his love for Linda and his
wish to please her, but it is the woman who replies flirtatiously,
and he grabs her and kisses her, while she thanks him for the
gifts of stockings. The woman's and Linda's laughter mingle as
the light leaves the woman and shines on Linda who, ironically,
is mending a pair of stockings.

  Willy and Linda continue their former conversation as though
there had been no break in it. Willy promises to make things up
to Linda and angrily tells her to stop mending stockings.
Bernard now enters with his tale of Biff's not studying and being

likely to fail. Willy tells Bernard that he will have to give Biff the answers in the examination, but Bernard says this is impossible in a state examination. Linda reminds Willy of the stolen football and adds that mothers are complaining of Biff's roughness with their daughters. Bernard adds more by revealing that Biff is driving the car without a licence and also that Biff's tutor says he is 'stuck up'. Willy is, at first, furious at Biff's shortcomings, but then defends him against this rush of accusations. Linda, almost in tears, leaves the room.

ads Advertisements.
Hartford A New England town, in Connecticut.

Revision questions on Act 1, episodes 1–4

1 What evidence is there so far of Willy's instability? (i.e. his 'living in two worlds', his contradictory attitudes to Biff, his lack of moral values).

2 Make an assessment of the characters of Biff and Happy from these early scenes, and examine the difference between them.

3 What use has Arthur Miller made so far of scenery, music, lighting effects and changes of time?

4 What is there to admire about Linda? Do you find anything to regret in her attitude to Willy?

Act, 1, episode 5, pp.31–41

We return to 'present-time'. Willy is alone in the kitchen talking to himself, still in 'past-time', worrying about Biff's stealing and trying to convince himself that he is in no way to blame. Happy enters and tries to calm Willy. Willy tells him of his near-accident in the car and then speaks of his elder brother, Ben, and tells Happy how this brother was an adventurous man who left home and made a fortune by the time he was twenty-one. Willy wishes he had accepted Ben's offer to join him. Then, in despair, he cries: 'The woods are burning! I can't drive a car!'

At this moment, Charley enters. He has obviously heard Willy, and, a kindly man, he fears for him and wants to help. Happy leaves and Charley and Willy start to play cards. Charley, knowing Willy's predicament, offers him a job in his firm, but Willy is too proud to accept and tells Charley not to insult him. Willy then voices his uncertainty over Biff's unsettled life and Charley tells him to forget it, and, trying to cheer Willy, praises his handiwork in putting up a ceiling in the living-room. Willy, in quarrelsome mood, answers rudely. Uncle Ben enters (unseen, of course, by Charley, since he is present only in Willy's mind) and Willy, in his over-wrought state, addresses his remarks half to Charley and half to Ben. Again the missed opportunity of not going to Alaska with Ben is stated. Ben asks questions about the past and Willy replies, and then, to cover his confusion, realizing that Charley must be wondering at his conversation, he aggressively accuses Charley of misplay. Charley, offended, leaves.

Time now changes to the past as Linda enters, 'as of old', and meets Ben. Ben tells of his career: how he left home when Willy was nearly four and intended to join their father in Alaska, but ended up in Africa where he made his fortune in four years. Ben next speaks of their father as a great, wild-hearted pioneer who drove a wagon right across the country, selling the flutes he made on the way. Willy is delighted that his boys hear about the fine stock they sprang from, and he encourages Biff to show his athletic upbringing by fighting Ben. But Ben trips him and poises his umbrella over his eye, warning him never to fight fair with a stranger. Linda is frightened by this somewhat sinister man. Willy, still trying to impress Ben with his boys' upbringing, encourages them to go and steal sand from a nearby building site and start rebuilding the stoop. Charley enters and warns Willy that they'll get into trouble stealing, but Willy ignores his advice. Bernard rushes in to say the watchman is chasing Biff. Ben, as usual, is in a hurry and, after telling Willy he is impressed by the boys, and boasting once more of his rapid rise to riches, he 'leaves'.

The woods are burning A metaphor from the great open spaces, it
  suggests a final catastrophe. If Willy cannot drive a car he will have no
  job.
laconic Using few words.
shoot To deal, and hence to play cards.
What do you keep comin' in here for Willy's continual rudeness to
  Charley is part of his defence mechanism. Charley is not personally
  attractive, not particularly well liked, and yet he is successful and Willy
  is not.
clean 'Broke', having no money left.

taking a pot The card game being played is casino. In this game taking a pot means capturing cards, for instance by matching one on the table to one in your hand.

That's my build Playing casino a player can build up a number of cards on the table and eventually win them.

Nebraska ... South Dakota Two states in the centre, obviously crossed by father's wagon.

Ketchikan A city in Alaska.

Ohio, Indiana, Michigan, Illinois Four American states bordering on the south of the Great Lakes.

Brooklyn One of the four boroughs of New York City.

front stoop A raised, uncovered platform before the entrance of a house.

knickers Knickerbockers, i.e. loose-fitting breeches, gathered in at the knee.

lumber Timber.

six-by-tens Six inches by ten inches, the dimensions of a cross section of the timber.

Where are the rest of your pants Willy is teasing Charley about his knickerbockers, which cease below the knee.

My New England man Charley has his own firm and his New England salesman finds it a difficult territory.

casino A card game in which eleven points is game, the ten of diamonds counting two points, and the two of spades one.

Act 1, episode 6, pp.41–8

Time changes to the present, and Linda, in a night-gown, comes in to try to get Willy to bed; but he is still living in the past and thinking with admiration of Ben. He sets out to take a walk whilst still in his bedroom slippers. Biff, in pyjamas, comes down, and then Happy. They ask Linda what can be done for Willy, and she makes it plain that they might have helped more, and sooner. She tells Biff that Willy is at his worst when he, Biff, comes home and she asks Biff why they are so hateful to each other. Biff says he is going to change his attitude. Linda asks him when he will settle down. She tells him that if he has no feeling for his father then he cannot have any for her. She says she loves Willy and will not have anyone upsetting him, so Biff had better make up his mind to show his father respect, or leave the house.

Biff tells Linda to stop making excuses for Willy, since he never had an ounce of respect for her. Happy denies this. Linda then speaks with pathos of Willy's predicament. He may be only an ordinary, common man, but he is a human being and something terrible is happening to him, and attention must be paid to his crisis. He has worked thirty-six years for a company which now takes his salary away and makes him work on a straight commission. He drives seven hundred miles there and seven hundred back and sells nothing. He has to borrow fifty dollars a week from Charley and pretend it is his pay. Linda ends her pathetic defence of Willy by attacking her sons for their indifference. She calls Happy a 'philandering bum', and asks Biff what happened to his love for his father. Biff is stung into retorting that he knows Willy is a fake, and, when asked what he means, refuses to explain.

Linda tells Biff that Willy is trying to kill himself; his car smashes are not accidents, and she has found a length of rubber tubing in the cellar which could be attached to the gas pipe. She ends in tears telling Biff that Willy's life is in his hands. Biff tries to calm her and promises he will stay at home and help, but says he just does not fit into the world of business. Happy says it is because he does not try to please people; he upsets them by doing stupid things like whistling in the elevator, and taking time off when he should be working. Biff asks Happy if he ever takes time off, and Happy replies that he does but he makes certain he has covered his tracks. Biff still feels he should be doing an open air job and not be stifled in 'this nuthouse of a city'.

fob A jewel attached to the watch-chain.
straight commission Earnings are a percentage of sales and no fixed salary accompanies them.
philandering bum A womanizing tramp.
chip in . . . for half my pay cheque Put half my earnings towards the house.
taking the line around Taking samples of goods around to buyers.
take a fade Leave work unofficially.

Act 1, episode 7, pp.48–54

Willy, who has heard some of the brothers' conversation, comes in and at once quarrels with Biff. Biff tries to placate him, tells him he is going to see his first employer, Oliver, tomorrow, to try to persuade him to set him up in business. At first, Willy scoffs at this idea and then Happy joins in with a plan that the two brothers should start a firm selling sporting goods, 'The Loman

Line', and advertise it by forming teams and competing. Willy is impressed. The whole family gloats over this day-dream. Willy advises Biff how to behave to Oliver. But the delight soon ends in a quarrel when Biff tells Willy not to yell at Linda. Willy leaves the room, *'beaten down, guilt ridden'*.

Linda begs Biff to be kind to Willy and go and say goodnight to him, which he does. Willy gives Biff more advice on how to win Oliver's backing. Happy, not to be out of the picture, tells Linda he is going to get married. Willy reminisces about Biff's play in the football championship while Linda hums a lullaby. In the kitchen, Biff discovers the length of rubber tubing and, looking in horror towards his father's room, he removes it and goes to bed.

Filene's ... the Hub ... Slattery's i.e. popular meeting-places for Boston's businessmen.

Spalding A famous baseball player who, with his brother, founded a firm of sports goods manufacturers.

Be quiet, fine, and serious ... Walk in with a big laugh Two completely opposite pieces of advice given by Willy within half a minute of each other.

beaten down, guilt ridden Another hint that Biff knows something discreditable about Willy.

bucks Dollars.

Greatest thing in the world for him was to bum around This attitude of Willy towards Biff is completely contradictory to his usual one.

I'm gonna get married, Mom Happy again trying so hard to get in the picture.

golden pool of light ... a blue flame beneath red coils Notice the most effective use of coloured stage lighting to heighten the mood. In Willy's imagination, Biff is the 'Golden Boy' bathed in this light, and, in sinister contrast, is the blue flame and red coil from behind which Biff draws out the suicide tubing.

Revision questions on Act 1, episodes 5–7

1 Show how Willy's swiftly alternating moods of great depression and optimism in these scenes further confirm the impression of his instability.

2 Why is Ben introduced into the play? Illustrate Miller's effective use of him.

3 What criticism of modern civilization in America is contained in these scenes?

4 What alternatives to 'the rat race' are suggested in these scenes? Why are they sometimes called the 'American Dream'?

Act 2, episode 1, pp.55–9

It is the following morning, and the scene opens happily with Willy having breakfast after a good night's sleep, and both he and Linda are optimistic about Biff's chance of persuading Oliver to back him in business. Willy talks of buying seeds on the way home, but Linda reminds him there is not enough light in the garden to grow anything. Willy promises to get a little place in the country and he will build extensions to it so that the boys can come and stay. Linda reminds Willy he is going to see his boss, Howard, today and persuade him to give him a job in the New York office. She adds that he should ask for a little salary in advance as they have bills to settle: the insurance premium, the final payment on the refrigerator, and on the mortgage for the house. Now, after twenty-five years, they will own the house.

Linda then tells Willy that he must meet his sons at Frank's Chop House at six as they are going to stand him a dinner. Willy leaves for work delighted. The phone rings: it is Biff to remind her to tell Willy about the dinner. She tells Biff with relief that the rubber gas tube has gone, but learns that it was not Willy who had discarded it but Biff who had removed it. However, she tells Biff how happily Willy had left for work, and begs Biff to be kind to his father at the dinner because he may have good news too.

take me off the road Give me a job which does not involve travelling.
grace period The time allowed between the date the payment of an instalment is due and the date on which the policy will be cancelled on account of failure to pay.
blow you Treat you.

Act 2, episode 2, pp.59–66

The scene changes to Howard Wagner's office. He is plugging in a wire-recorder as Willy enters, keyed up to ask his employer for an office job. But he is not given the chance for some minutes as Howard is intent on demonstrating his new 'toy' and revelling in the recordings he has made of his family talking and whistling. Willy has to listen. Suddenly Howard asks him why he is not in

Boston working. Willy says that that is what he has come to see him about. He asks for a job in New York, but Howard points out that it is a road business and there are only a few office jobs and they are filled. Willy, pathetically, reminds Howard that he was with the firm when Howard was a babe in his father's arms, and says he needs no more than fifty dollars a week. But Howard is adamant.

Willy then tells Howard, at length, how he came to be a salesman instead of setting out to Alaska with his elder brother. He speaks of meeting an eighty-four-year-old salesman named Dave Singleman, whom he admired greatly for his personality, which enabled him to pick up a phone and call buyers everywhere; and when he died hundreds of salesmen and buyers were at his funeral. Therefore Willy decided selling was the life for him. But now, he says, it has all changed; personality and friendship count for nothing. Howard agrees but refuses Willy's offer to work for him for only forty dollars a week. When Willy starts quoting Howard's father, Howard impatiently leaves the office, telling Willy to pull himself together.

Left alone, Willy stares at Howard's vacated chair, which is now strangely lit, and imagines he sees Frank Wagner, Howard's father, who first employed Willy. He leans forward appealing to him and accidentally switches on the recorder, which gives a recitation of the capital cities of American states by Howard's son. Willy shouts out in fright and Howard rushes in and pulls out the plug. Willy, abandoning all hope of persuading Howard to give him an office job, says he will go to Boston. Howard now tells Willy he does not want him to represent the firm any more. In answer to Willy's pathetic appeals, he tells him to ask his own sons for help. Howard leaves the office telling Willy to return his samples during the week.

wire-recording machine The forerunner of the tape-recorder.
She's crazy for me Notice the parallel between Howard and Willy in their relationships with their children.
The capital city of Howard's son is reciting the capital cities of the American states in alphabetical order.
Bulova watch time A quotation from a radio commercial.
bandsaw A mechanical saw. Carpentry was one of Willy's hobbies.
Jack Benny Famous American comedian (d. 1976).
a half-dozen salesmen on the floor here The firm consists of travellers and has only a few salesmen at headquarters in New York.

set my table Enable me to exist.

hundreds of salesmen ... funeral Remember this and compare it to
Willy's own funeral.

Al Smith Democratic Presidential candidate, 1928. Defeated by
Republican, Herbert Hoover.

the light ... grows very bright and strange Notice this use of lighting
to suggest Willy's hallucination.

Act 2, episode 3, pp.66–70

Willy is left alone in Howard's office. We return with Willy to the
past as Ben's music is heard and he enters – returning from
Alaska and calling to say good-bye before departing again for
faraway places. Willy asks Ben to help him and Ben offers him a
job as overseer of his forests in Alaska. Linda enters, and,
hearing Ben's proposition, is frightened and encourages Willy to
play safe and stay a salesman. She reminds Willy of the success
of Dave Singleman. Biff enters in his high school sweater with
Happy who carries his gear for him. Willy proudly shows off
Biff to Ben, boasting that three universities want him and that
he is bound to succeed in business, because success depends
entirely on being well liked. Ben reminds Willy of his Alaska
offer and then departs. Bernard enters and competes with
Happy to carry Biff's football gear. It is the great football game
this afternoon which, according to Willy, is going to make Biff
captain of the All-Scholastic Championship Team of New York.
Biff promises to score a touch-down especially for his father. As
they leave excitedly, Charley enters and, for a laugh, pretends
he does not know the game is on. Instead of a laugh he gets a
snubbing from an angry Willy.

music Notice again the use of music as an extra dimension.

pennants Flags to show support of their team.

locker room Changing room. Notice Ebbets Field boasts a clubhouse,
not mere changing rooms.

Room? For what? Charley first pretends he does not know there is an
important game on. Next he pretends it is baseball, knowing full well it
is the football season. Then he invents a newsflash that Ebbets Field
just blew up, and, returning to the baseball leg-pull, he exhorts Biff to
knock a homer (hit the ball hard and accurately enough to enable him
to complete the circuit and return to base, as in 'rounders'.) Finally he
pretends he has never heard of Red Grange, the famous American
football player, known as 'The Galloping Ghost' for his spectacular
feats.

Act 2, episode 4, pp.70–8

The scene changes to the reception room of Charley's office, and time to the present. Willy has been fired by Howard and has now come to borrow more money from Charley. Bernard is in the office. He has become a successful lawyer. Jenny, his father's secretary, comes to tell him that Willy is arguing with himself in the corridor, and she cannot manage him. Willy enters and is surprised to see Bernard, who is off to Washington on a law case. They greet each other; then Bernard asks after Biff, and Willy lies about his 'successful' career in the West and his big deal with Oliver. Willy, obviously impressed by Bernard's success, asks him, with emotion, the secret of it and, then, completely reversing his account of Biff, he admits that he has been a failure ever since that unsuccessful maths examination at seventeen, and he asks Bernard why he thinks this is. Bernard, in turn, asks Willy if anything happened between him and Biff at Boston at that time. Willy is now resentful and on the defensive.

Charley enters, and tells Willy that Bernard is about to defend a case in the Supreme Court. Willy is most impressed and asks why Bernard had not told him about it. The difference between the two families is summarized when Charley replies: 'He don't have to – he's gonna do it' – action is not words. Willy, puzzled, remarks to Charley that he had never told Bernard what to do, and Charley replies that his salvation is that he never took an interest in anything. He then hands over the fifty dollars he knows he has come to borrow. Willy, with difficulty, explains that he has his insurance to pay and needs a hundred and ten dollars.

Charley repeats to Willy his offer of a job, and asks him why he won't work for him. Willy furiously refuses the offer and is ready to fight Charley for the 'insult'. But Charley treats him kindly, and Willy confesses that he has just been fired by the man he had helped name as a baby. Charley points out that sentiment means nothing and that being well liked is not the answer. In his forthright, practical way he adds: 'The only thing you got in this world is what you can sell!' But Willy still refuses Charley's offer of a job and Charley gives Willy the extra money he has asked for. Willy remarks, thinking of his life insurance, that it is funny one ends up worth more dead than alive. Charley, sounding a warning, tells Willy, 'Nobody's worth nothin' dead.' Willy, on the verge of tears, tells Charley he is the only friend he has got.

carte blanche Having power to decide as he wishes.
argue Defend.
My salvation is that I never took any interest in anything Charley, unlike Willy, believes in deeds rather than words. What he is saying is that he did not, like Willy, continually fill his son's head with false ideals and flattery.
strapped 'Broke', bankrupt.
J. P. Morgan Famous American banker, known as the 'Jupiter' of American finance. Charley is syaing that he was liked for his money rather than his personality.

Act 2, episode 5, pp.78–91

The scene changes to a restaurant. Stanley, a waiter, is preparing a table for Happy, who orders an expensive meal, telling Stanley it is to celebrate a big deal his brother is pulling off. A lavishly dressed call-girl enters and Happy proceeds to stand her champagne and flirt with her. When Biff comes in he introduces him to the girl telling her he is a great football player and suggests she phone for a friend to make a foursome. The two brothers left alone, Biff tells Happy what happened at Oliver's. He waited six hours in vain for an interview, and, when Oliver left at five, he approached him but was not remembered.

Biff faces the truth: he never had been a salesman with Oliver, only a shipping clerk, and he realizes what a lie his whole life has been. Before leaving Oliver's he stole his fountain pen and is filled with remorse at this crazy action. He asks Happy to help him convince Willy when he comes that his dream of him as potentially great is an illusion. Happy, preferring the illusion, encourages Biff to tell lies about the interview to keep his father happy. Willy enters and Biff, slightly drunk by now, orders double whiskeys. He starts to tell his father of his interview. He points out he was never a salesman, only a clerk. Willy is in no mood for further bad news and announces that he has just been fired.

He questions Biff on his interview with Oliver and Happy repeatedly interrupts with his lies, trying to prevent Biff telling of his complete failure. Biff is just giving up in angry despair when we return to the past and hear Bernard knocking frantically on the door, calling for Mrs Loman. This, of course, is happening only in Willy's mind, and meanwhile Biff begins to tell the true story of his interview. The past in Willy's mind supersedes the present; Bernard announces to Linda that Biff has failed his mathematics examination and they believe he has gone to Boston to find his father.

Present time, as it were, gradually returns and Willy realizes Biff is telling him of the afternoon's failure and the stealing of the pen. This has such a stunning effect on Willy that he now imagines that he is being summoned to his office, first by an operator's voice, and then a page boy's announcements. He shouts wildly back, in between condemnations of Biff's worthlessness. Biff is now frightened, and to calm his father pretends that he is to have lunch with Oliver the next day, and that all is not lost. But he cannot keep up this pretence and soon tells his father that he has no lunch appointment. A woman's voice is heard laughing off-stage. Willy accuses Biff of spiting him and then hits Biff, and as Happy is separating them, the call-girls come in.

While Willy is reliving an incident in the past with the woman, who keeps telling him there is someone at the door, the boys talk to the girls. Willy rises to his feet saying he is going to open the door, and then asks the bemused Biff where the washroom is. Biff directs him to it. When Willy has left, Happy forgets him and starts to arrange the evening ahead, but Biff is in no mood for this. He blames Happy for doing nothing to save Willy's life. He produces the rubber gas tubing and, ready to weep, he hurries out. Happy explains to the girls that Biff is just a bit overstrung, and hurries the girls after him. When one of them asks him if he is not going to tell his father what is happening he denies that Willy is his father.

raucous music ... red glow Notice how music and light are again used to suggest the atmosphere of the scene.

Hackensack A suburb of New York. Used here, ironically, as a backward area.

hit a number Draw a winning number in a lottery.

Strudel Pastry often filled with apple, used here as slang for a pretty girl. Compare 'a peach' or even a 'piece of crumpet'.

binoculars Eyes.

cover girl Photographer's model for the covers of magazines.

quarterback ... New York Giants He plays as one of the backs for this New York football team which is a member of the National Football League of America.

West Point The American Military Academy, compare British Sandhurst.

no soap No luck.

Let's get a load on Let's fill ourselves up with drink.

bullin' around Telling lies.

the woods are burning A picturesque metaphor from the wide open spaces suggesting time is running out and a crisis is upon them.

trumpet note . . . light of green leaves The music and colour represent the past. Willy's mind, frightened by the thought that Biff's interview with Oliver has been a failure, now imagines Biff's earlier failure and relives Bernard's announcement of Biff's failure in his exam.

graduate him Give him the necessary qualifications to enter university.

Grand Central New York's main railway station.

OPERATOR'S VOICE Willy's thoroughly overwrought brain imagines it hears an announcer calling for him on the public address system.

PAGE'S VOICE The imaginary operator is apparently unsuccessful in calling Willy and now he imagines a messenger boy has been sent round to call for him.

THE WOMAN The critical scene of the past between Willy, Biff, and the woman with whom Willy has been staying, is about to be staged. Miller cleverly introduces it by these hallucinations of Willy's intermingled with the dialogue of the restaurant scene.

Willy's state of exhaustion and his mingling of past with present is obviously growing in this scene. His self-delusion alternates with moments of truth in his attitude to his own predicament and Biff's. The love-hate relationship between Willy and Biff is predominant. Willy at times deceives himself into thinking Biff is so certain to succeed, and at others is telling him that he is no good for anything. He actually strikes him in his angry frustration. Biff now, unlike Happy, wishes to face the truth about himself and make his father face it too; but he is unable to communicate with him.

Happy's lack of ethics in his wishing to prolong his father's illusions about Biff's interview, and in his lies to the call girls, and Biff's theft of Oliver's pen, reflect their upbringing.

Revision questions on Act 2, episodes 1–5

1 Describe Willy and Biff's attempts to improve their lot in life by seeking interviews, and comment on the results.

2 What evidence is there in these scenes of the philosophy that outward appearances count more than anything for success. What is meant by 'success', as seen by Willy?

3 Discuss the contrast in these scenes between Willy and Biff on one side, and Charley and Bernard on the other.

4 Describe the scene in the restaurant in some detail, emphasizing the difference in attitude shown by the two sons to their father.

Act 2, episode 6, pp.91–7

The scene is an apartment in Boston, in the past. Willy is remembering. He has been making love to his woman and, in the middle of the night, is disturbed by insistent knocking on the door. Willy makes the woman hide in the bathroom and returns to find Biff has entered the room. He confesses to his father that he failed his mathematics examination and begs his father to see his tutor and persuade him to change the result. Willy agrees at once and Biff is delightedly reassured. Then comes the critical moment in their relationship: Biff hears the woman laugh in the bathroom, and then, as she enters, stares at her 'open-mouthed and horrified'. Willy quickly pretends it is someone from a nearby room who has come in to use his shower because her own is being decorated. He introduces her to Biff as a buyer, but she prevents any pretence by asking for her clothes, which are in the bedroom, and by reminding Willy that he promised her a present of stockings. She then goes out with the stockings.

Willy tries to ignore the whole incident but by now Biff is in tears. Willy tries pretence again but, realizing that this is useless, tries to tell Biff that he must not over-emphasize things, that he will see them differently when he grows up. He tells Biff he will see the tutor in the morning. But Biff now rejects the whole idea of graduating and going to university and accuses his father of giving this stranger stockings which should have been given to his mother. Willy angrily orders Biff to stop crying, but Biff turns on him, calling him a 'phony little fake', then leaves, overcome with tears.

This is the crux of the relationship between father and son. From now on Biff becomes a waster and cannot forget his father's deceit. Willy's attitude to Biff changes: in self defence, he goes over to the attack.

Willy is on his knees shouting to his son to obey his order and come back, when the scene changes back to the restaurant and the present time, and Willy is shouting to the waiter. Stanley helps Willy to his feet and tells him that his sons have left with the call girls. Willy says he can get home by himself, tips Stanley and asks if there is a seed shop in the neighbourhood as he has nothing planted in the garden. (Here Willy, in desperation, is clinging to the legend of 'the natural life', and thinks of buying seeds.)

Raw, sensuous music Again emphasizing the nature of the scene.
sheers Fine stockings. Notice the important use of the stockings. We have seen Willy hurt by the signs of Linda mending stockings (no wonder!), and now they are to become the focal point of Biff's disillusionment with his father.

Act 2, episode 7, pp.97–109

The sons return home from their evening with the call girls. Linda is waiting and when Happy gives her a bunch of roses, she knocks them to the floor and, ignoring him, turns to Biff and accuses him of not caring if his father dies. Biff says he wants to see his father. Linda upbraids them for their callous neglect of their father in the restaurant and orders them out of the house for ever. She calls Biff a louse and Biff, disgusted with himself, agrees remorsefully with her accusations. Linda refuses to let him see Willy, but Biff, attracted by a noise outside, discovers Willy sowing vegetable seeds by torchlight in the garden. As he sows, Willy holds an imaginary conversation with Ben. He asks Ben for his advice on his plan to commit suicide so that Biff can receive the life insurance money. Ben, at first, warns him the company might not honour the policy and adds that it is a coward's way out. When Willy, in reply, asks Ben if it is less cowardly to stay alive making no money, Ben thinks again. Willy then compares his plan to becoming rich by discovering a diamond, and tells Ben that it will change Biff's attitude towards him, from contempt to admiration. He imagines his own funeral crowded with representatives from the New England states, and what an eye-opener it will be for Biff. Ben says Biff will only call him a coward and hate him. To the accompaniment of the boys' music, Willy thinks of the happy times in the past and asks Ben why he cannot give Biff something, and so help to stop his son's hatred. Ben says he must think again about Willy's plan as he drifts out of sight.

Biff approaches Willy as he confusedly tries to sow seeds. He tells his father he has come to say goodbye. He has found the truth about himself although he cannot explain this to Willy. They go into the house and Linda agrees that Biff is right to go away. Biff asks his father to shake hands but Willy is still thinking of Biff's supposed appointment with Oliver the next day. He refuses to shake hands and, as Biff attempts to leave, he stops him and curses him and tells him that all he has done has been out of spite. Biff denies this and, in desperation, calls his father a phony and produces the piece of rubber gas tube. Willy disclaims it. Biff is determined now to face the truth and make his father see it too.

When Happy interrupts, he challenges his illusion that he is the assistant buyer by pointing out that he is only one of two assistants to the assistant. And then Biff confesses: he stole in Kansas City and was in jail; in fact, he lost every job he had through stealing. He blames his father for bringing him up to believe he was so wonderful that he could never take orders from anybody. He says that he suddenly realized his own life's falsity as he was leaving Oliver's with the stolen pen. He tells Willy he is no hero, just an ordinary being, and faces his father with the fact that he too is ordinary. Willy cannot take this idea – 'I am Willy Loman, and you are Biff Loman!' Biff angrily tells Willy they are neither of them leaders. Willy accuses Biff of saying all this in spite and he starts up the stairs in fright expecting Biff to attack him.

But this is the climax and instead, Biff breaks down sobbing, holding on to Willy, who dumbly fumbles for Biff's face. When Biff, broken and in tears, leaves the room, the astonished Willy is suddenly strangely elevated. 'Isn't that – isn't that remarkable? Biff – he likes me!' But he has only discovered half the truth – he still clings to his dream: ' – that boy is going to be magnificent!' And, in his imagination, Ben answers him – yes, with Willy's life insurance money to back him Biff will succeed.

Happy, at this moment, makes a desperate effort to get some notice taken of him by announcing he is going to get married and change everything. Linda tries to get Willy to go to bed but, with Ben's tempting words about diamonds in the jungle sounding in his imagination, Willy says he wants to stay down for a little while and persuades Linda to go upstairs on her own. He continues talking to Ben, rejoicing in his plan to ensure Biff's success by his own death. Now his mind goes back to the afternoon of the great ball-game and he is giving Biff advice. Then Linda calls him from upstairs, but his mind is in a whirl and, to the sound of an intensely high-pitched note of music, resembling an unbearable scream, he rushes out of the house. There is the noise of the car speeding off and the music crashing down in a frenzy of sound. This music then changes to a funeral march and the scene dissolves into a graveyard.

the sound of the flute Music again denotes the change of episode.
blue of night Colour helps indicate the mood.
proposition Willy's suicide plan to get the insurance money for Biff.
on the barrelhead An immediate cash payment.
gilt-edged Absolutely safe.
ringing up a zero Scoring nothing, therefore being a failure financially.
gay music Music again used to help the audience share Willy's emotions.
rap Blame.
dime a dozen Two-a-penny (old pence too!)
drummer Salesman.
ash-can Dustbin.
seventy yard boot Kick the ball seventy yards.
music ... scream ... music crashes down ... soft pulsation ... dead march Notice how important the music is in helping the dialogue and action to communicate the panic and terror of the final climax.

Requiem, pp.110–12

The scene at the grave follows directly from the last episode. Each of the main characters summarizes his or her reaction to Willy's suicide. Happy begins by expressing his anger at an unnecessary action, saying, 'We would've helped him.' Linda is bewildered because only the immediate family and Charley and Bernard have come to the funeral, and she cannot understand why Willy did it just when all the hire-purchase instalments were completed. Charley answers her by saying, 'No man only needs a little salary.' Biff looks back to the happy days when his father enjoyed making things round the house and says, 'He had the wrong dreams. All, all wrong.' Charley gives his opinion that it was the job which was to blame: a salesman's life is insecure, he can lose his popularity and with it his job. But Biff assures Charley, 'Charley, the man didn't know who he was'. He asks Happy to come away from the city with him, but Happy denies that his father had the wrong dream and declares that he is going to prove it by being a success himself.

Biff tries to get Linda to leave the grave, but she asks to be left alone for a minute to say goodbye to Willy. To the sounds of the flute music she makes her pathetic farewell. She cannot understand why he did it when they were at last free of debts; the house is theirs, 'and there'll be nobody home.' Sobbing quietly, she allows Biff to take her away.

But where are all the people he knew? Compare this with Willy's dream of his own funeral.

no rock bottom to the life There is no real security to the job.

riding on a smile and a shoeshine A pleasant metaphor, implying that so much depends on a pleasant personality and appearance.

The flute begins Imagine how the music would heighten the pathos of Linda's farewell.

Revision questions on episodes 6, 7 and Requiem

1 Describe the scene at Boston when Willy is surprised by Biff. What lasting effect does this have on (a) Biff, (b) Willy.

2 Examine the relationship between Willy and Biff in these last scenes.

3 What evidence is there in these scenes that Biff has learned the truth about himself?

4 Examine the different attitudes to Willy's suicide as shown by each of the main characters in 'Requiem'.

The characters

Willy Loman

He had the wrong dreams. All, all, wrong.

Willy Loman *is* the play. A complete understanding of him will
help solve any dilemma we may have as to whether he is a 'tragic
hero' or 'a little man as victim', and that, in turn, will help to
decide whether the play is a tragedy or a social commentary,
whether it can rank as 'great' or 'commonplace'. We are helped
in this understanding by the author's intense interest in his
protagonist; we do, in fact, enter into Willy's mind and it is no
surprise that Arthur Miller's first title for the play was 'The
Inside of his Head'.

As we go through the play we shall look for illustrations of
Willy's characteristics. The first of these must be his compulsion
to live a lie. He is usually unable to differentiate between fact
and fancy, so impulsively has he chosen illusion rather than
reality. From this first character trait spring others: his errors in
judgment and his moral lapses. Because of this he loses his real
identity and becomes a lonely, helpless individual. We have to
study the outward causes of his sickness of mind: the oppression
and frustration inherent in modern society. Finally – and this is
perhaps his strongest claim to the epithet 'tragic' rather than to
the lesser one, 'pathetic' – we must recognize the intensity with
which he strives to match his dream.

Even before the dialogue begins, Miller indicates Willy's weary
condition, in the stage directions. He is carrying heavy cases of
samples with difficulty: *'Even as he crosses the stage to the doorway of
the house, his exhaustion is apparent.'*

The opening episode, in which Willy surprises his wife, Linda, by
an unexpectedly early return from a business trip, emphasizes
this exhaustion. 'I'm tired to the death,' he says, and explains
that he could not drive beyond the outskirts of the city because
the car kept going off the road. The episode also gives us the
first hints of Willy's self-deception: he declares he is a 'vital'
salesman. We soon see his antagonistic attitude to his elder son,

Biff, and this is the first thread of a major pattern in the play; it appears to be directed against his inability to settle and 'get on' in life. Much later we realize there is far more to it than this. Further evidence of his mental exhaustion comes in his habit of contradicting himself – Biff is a 'lazy bum' one moment, and the next: 'There's one thing about Biff – he's not lazy.'

His tired mind makes him readily irritable over minor details such as whipped cheese. The recurring motif of his being stifled by over-population begins here, as does his frustration at the system which forces him to slave all his life to pay off mortgages. The flashbacks occur in Willy's mind only and are symptomatic of his approaching breakdown. They also, of course, illustrate his false philosophy of life and its effect on his sons as he indoctrinates them with his code. The stealing of a football will be condoned because the thief is popular. Biff will be much more successful than hard-working Bernard because Biff is liked. And through it all we constantly hear Willy boasting of his own popularity and his consequent success as a salesman – facts which prove to be fiction when we get to know him. 'I did five hundred gross in Providence and seven hundred gross in Boston' – soon reduced to truth by Linda's questioning. There swiftly follows one of those moments when Willy passes from fantasy to truth and, filled with self-pity, admits he is a failure – too fat, too talkative.

Willy's duplicity is revealed early in the play. Just when he is telling Linda how important she is to him we have a flashback to Willy and his mistress in Boston.

We are helped to understand Willy better in his scene with Charley. His attitude to Charley is really based on jealousy. Charley is a business success, yet has none of the qualities Willy admires. He is liked but not well-liked; he is not athletic, nor is he practical – he cannot even hammer a nail in, according to Willy, who puts up ceilings and builds stoops. So Willy, his pride at stake, angrily refuses any job Charley offers him in his own firm.

Ben, Willy's elder brother who appears only in Willy's imagination, gives us a further insight into Willy's character. Ben represents Willy's daydream of getting rich quickly by an adventurous life – finding diamonds in the jungle. He also makes a good audience for Willy's delight in the way he has brought up his sons to be 'rugged, well-liked', and he encourages them to steal timber from a building site to impress Ben with their supposedly courageous and adventurous natures.

Towards the end of Act 1, Linda's fierce defence of Willy and her attack on her sons for their indifference to their father's fate establishes Willy's pathetic predicament fully. After a cry to Biff, 'Why are you so hateful to each other?', she speaks at length and highly emotionally of Willy's condition. We learn that he no longer earns a salary from his firm, but is working on a straight commission, like a beginner; that he often travels seven hundred miles and sells nothing, that he borrows fifty dollars a week from Charley to keep up the pretence that he is earning a living. Worst of all, we hear that Linda believes his car accidents to be deliberate attempts at suicide and that, furthermore, she has discovered a hidden piece of tubing in the cellar with a new connection on the gas pipe. In an emotional appeal, Linda establishes the pathos of Willy's plight: 'He's not the finest character that ever lived. But he's a human being, and a terrible thing is happening to him. So attention must be paid. He's not to be allowed to fall into his grave like an old dog.'

In the last eposode of Act 1, Biff and Happy dream up their idea of starting their own firm. Willy is delighted: 'You guys together could absolutely lick the civilized world.' His advice to Biff, who is to approach his first employer to sponsor them, is full of contradictions '... don't crack any jokes', he says, and, 'Walk in very serious.' But a little later he is saying, 'Start off with a couple of your good stories to lighten things up.' His advice, on this occasion, is as usual full of his shallow philosophy, that appearances count more than intrinsic worth. 'It's not what you say, it's how you say it — because personality always wins the day.'

The act closes with Willy revelling in a memory of Biff bathed in golden light, like a young god on the football field: 'A star like that, magnificent, can never really fade away!' he comments in the ecstasy of his self-deception.

The second act finds Willy still filled with optimism. He is confident that his employer will take him off the road and give him a headquarters job in New York. Biff is going to succeed in persuading Oliver to sponsor him. The boys have planned a dinner to celebrate. Willy, in his excited mood, turns to thoughts of buying seeds for the garden, closing his eyes to the fact that the soil is sterile. He thinks of buying a place in the country where he can enjoy the pastime that he really seems to excel at – building and making things with his hands. This is a typically sad pipe-dream of Willy's which, like the rest, is never fulfilled.

The interview with his employer is, inevitably, a failure. The pathos of Willy literally begging from the younger man is heightened by Willy's long, sentimental explanation of why he became a salesman. As a youth he had met an 84-year-old salesman who was 'remembered and loved and helped by so many different people' so that he simply went to the phone in his room, at that age, and called the buyers. That salesman, when he died, had hundreds of others attending his funeral.

Willy regrets the changes time has wrought in business. 'There was respect, and comradeship, and gratitude in it. Today, it's all cut and dried, and there's no chance for bringing friendship to bear – or personality.' This is a revealing passage. No doubt there is truth in Willy's statement. As civilization becomes yearly more complex, so the machine supersedes human relationships – the computer is unlikely to be 'remembered and loved' – but can Willy truthfully blame his predicament entirely on social changes? Is not the seed of his failure contained within himself? He has admitted earlier that he has become too fat and talkative and is no longer well liked. Again and again we have seen him mistake the outward trimmings of personality, based on good looks and popularity, for the intrinsic worth of character which inspires friendship and love. This blind self-delusion, accompanied by his intense determination to maintain the false image, leads to his destruction and is the stuff of tragedy.

His employer fires him. Willy, left alone, exhausted, returns in his mind to the past. Ben is there, and at once we hear further evidence of this blind self-delusion of Willy's. He tells Ben that three great universities are begging for Biff and attributes this to having contacts, not to any real worth: 'It's who you know and the smile on your face!'

Willy calls on Charley to borrow more money. He comes from the lift talking to himself about that ball-game of old. Reading the play, one does not always realize the extent of Willy's deterioration as clearly as one would – here, for example – in the audience, watching Bernard and Jenny's anxiety and embarrassment at Willy's peculiar behaviour. Talking to Bernard, he displays the wishful thinking we have come to recognize as his lifeline: Biff has been doing great things in the West and now his former employer wants him badly. Willy is greatly impressed by Bernard's success which he seems to measure by superficial standards – his friends have a private tennis court! Then comes one of his sudden moments of truth. Pathetically, he asks Bernard what is the secret of his success and admits that Biff is a failure. We are prepared for that later scene in Boston by Bernard's asking what happened there to alter the whole of Biff's life, and by Willy's guilty evasion. Bernard touches the nerve-ends of Willy's plight in the following dialogue:

Bernard . . . Goodbye, Willy, and don't worry about it. You know, 'If at first you don't succeed . . .'
Willy Yes, I believe in that.
Bernard But sometimes, Willy, it's better for a man just to walk away.
Willy Walk away?
Bernard That's right.
Willy But if you can't walk away?
Bernard (*after a slight pause*) I guess that's when it's tough. (*Extending his hand*) Goodbye, Willy.

Bernard leaves and Willy asks Charley for the loan, confessing that he has been fired by Howard, whom he had known since a baby and whose Christian name he had helped to choose. Charley pours cold water on this when replying, 'The only thing you got in this world is what you can sell.' And when Willy repeats his code of the necessity to be impressive and well-liked, Charley cuts him short by telling him that the only reason the famous and wealthy were 'liked' was for their money.

The restaurant scene follows, and Willy senses immediately that Biff has not been successful with Oliver, but refuses to allow himself to accept this. He first tells of his own failure, will not listen to Biff's attempt to tell the truth about his and interrupts him continually with optimistic comments based entirely on his wishful thinking. Then, unable to sustain this self-deception any longer, he loses his temper with Biff and, in his anguished mind, imagining he is with his mistress in Boston, he is led by Biff to the washroom, where he collapses.

The scene in which Biff discovers his father's infidelity follows. It is a pathetic liaison with a woman, an outcome of his longing to be liked and of his inability to find complete satisfaction from his relationship with his wife because he tried too hard to hide his failure from her. Willy now makes a futile attempt to conceal this liaison from his son. It is the turning point in their relationship. From now on Biff surrenders to failure and Willy, laden with guilt in his son's presence, tries to defend himself by accusing Biff of spite.

Willy is by now facing a complete breakdown. On his way home from the restaurant he buys seeds and, when the boys arrive home, Biff discovers him sowing them in the sterile soil of their yard by torchlight. It is the primitive longing in him for the simple life free from all the complexities of earning a living in an industrial age. Cleverly, the author shows us the growth of another seed in Willy's mind. Suicide has already been anticipated by the car crashes and the gas tubing and now it is coming to the forefront of Willy's mind.

Ben reappears in his imagination and he discusses with him the pros and cons of killing himself, rather in the way that Shakespeare used soliloquies – for instance, Macbeth's before murdering Duncan – to show the inner workings of the mind. Willy sees his suicide as a means of setting Biff on the road to success with the insurance money and, more important still, of gaining his respect once more. But the saner half of Willy's mind, represented by Ben at this stage, counsels against a stupid act: the insurance company might not pay; it is a cowardly action; Biff will only hate him. To counter this he thinks of the twenty thousand dollars as a diamond waiting to be picked up and, furthermore, what a funeral he will have with representatives coming from all over New England and New York: Biff will be so impressed. Willy is completely obsessed by the thought of regaining Biff's love. He pines for the happy days of old when Biff loved him, and his heart-cry, 'Why, why can't I give him something and not have him hate me?', touches even Ben who says he must rethink the situation.

Biff then enters and tells Willy he is leaving because he cannot make him understand the truth that he, Biff, is not a potential world-wonder – he is a bum. Willy, in his blindness, will have none of this and is angry with Biff. He will not even shake his hand before he goes, cursing him instead. It is an act of self-destruction. His only hope of a reconciliation with Biff would be to accept the truth about them both; but he wilfully closes his eyes to this and buries his head in the sand of his hopelessly wrong dreams. When he still accuses Biff of trying to destroy him through spite, Biff is driven to a desperate act to try to show Willy the error of his ways: he produces the gas tubing, then tells his father of his own futile career of petty theft – he blames his father bitterly for bringing him up on the 'hot air' of flattery and impossible dreams. He cries, 'Pop! I'm a dime a dozen, and so are you!' Willy, still true to his dream, insists, 'I am not a dime a dozen! I am Willy Loman, and you are Biff Loman!' Again Biff tries to make him see the truth; but in a moment of intense pathos the crisis comes – Biff breaks down sobbing, holding on to Willy. He begs him to burn his 'phony dream before something happens'. Willy, at last, sees part of the truth: Biff likes him. He is astonished, elevated; for a moment there seems a chance of a happy ending to the play but this is quickly shattered.

Willy That boy – that boy is going to be magnificent!
Ben Yes, outstanding, with twenty thousand behind him.

From now on, Willy's mind is filled with two thoughts – the fact that Biff has always loved him, and his determination to set Biff on the road to success by killing himself. With these thoughts he goes to his death.

In the 'Requiem', Biff pinpoints Willy's tragedy – 'He never knew who he was.' He lived a false dream. The seeds of his self-destruction were in him from the start. It is not enough to say that Willy was just a 'little man as victim'; although one can sympathize with his hatred of the stifling conditions of a modern industrial society, those conditions are only incidentally to blame for his tragedy. It is true that he behaves extremely stupidly, but then so did Othello, King Lear and many other tragic 'heroes'. Stupidity does not preclude tragedy.

The dynamic whole-heartedness of Willy's bid for love and success, and the intensity of his pathetic struggle, make him a 'tragic hero' to this reader's mind – but you must decide for yourself.

Biff

Pop, I'm nothing! I'm nothing, Pop. Can't you understand that?

Biff Loman is an important character, so much so that some readers, or members of the audience, particularly younger ones, identify themselves with him in his relationship with his father and consider that he is the protagonist of the play rather than Willy Loman. Arthur Miller, in his Introduction to his *Collected Plays*, implies that there are two main systems at conflict in the play: the first, Willy's anxiety that he has broken the law of society which states that success is essential in order to belong, and the second, the opposing system '. . . which, so to speak, is in a race for Willy's faith, and it is the system of love which is the opposite of the law of success. It is embodied in Biff Loman . . .'

On a first reading of the play we find it hard to believe in the strength of any love between father and son: from the very start their antagonism is underlined. Linda, in the opening scene, tells Willy he must not criticize Biff so much and lose his temper with him, and Willy cries, 'Biff is a lazy bum!'

We discover that Biff is thirty-four and that he has had a restless, rootless life. As school he excelled at athletics, particularly football, but neglected his studies. He failed mathematics in his attempt to qualify for university and, rather than take a second chance and re-take the subject, he gave up the idea of university, left school and became a shipping clerk. This led nowhere; he stole a carton of basket-balls from his employer, then left the firm to avoid being fired. After that he admits to working at twenty to thirty different jobs, ending as a farmhand in the West for the last ten years. He also admits to serving a gaol sentence of three months in Kansas City for stealing a suit, and he cries, 'I stole myself out of every job since High School!' He is usually under no illusions about his life: '. . . I know that all I've done is to waste my life . . . I'm mixed up very bad.'

This is not exactly an endearing summary of his first thirty-four years, except for the honesty of the last admissions, and that virtue, as we shall see, is all-important in its contrast to the self-delusions of others in the play.

There are as well certain mitigating circumstances in the play which help to explain, and perhaps partially excuse, Biff's behaviour. The strongest of these is his father's dream for him. It may be understandable for a father to have ambitions for his son but, when we study Willy's character, we realize that these ambitions have become part of his obsession with unreality; his life, in fact, is one big lie and, as we return again and again in the play to the past, we see the father encouraging the son by flattery and bringing him up to enter the same world of illusion where superficial qualities count for everything.

When Biff has 'borrowed' a ball from school and Happy, realizing it is unlikely to be returned, tells Biff he knew his father would not like this, Willy supports Biff's action: 'Coach'll probably congratulate you on your initiative! . . . That's because he likes you.'

When Bernard warns Willy that Biff will probably fail his exam through lack of study, Willy unethically orders Bernard: 'you'll give him the answers.'

It is interesting to hear Biff actually echo his father's words in his appraisal of Bernard: 'He's liked, but he's not well liked', a phrase used a few minutes before by Willy to describe Charley, clearly illustrating that Willy's philosophy is being effectively absorbed by Biff.

Further explanation of Biff's failure is given in the scene where he accidentally discovers his father's infidelity. Having failed his mathematics exam, he hurries to his father, who is on his rounds in Boston. Willy is comforting him in his hotel by telling him he will see his tutor at once and talk him into passing him, when a woman comes out of the bathroom into Willy's room. Biff stares at her 'open-mouthed and horrified'. Willy tries to get rid of the woman but she demands the promised gift of two boxes of stockings from him. Biff remembers how his mother is always mending her old stockings and, through his tears, he cries, 'You – you gave her Mama's stockings!' He leaves his father, shouting, 'You fake! You phony little fake! You fake!'

From that moment the relationship between Willy and Biff changes. Biff, badly shaken, completely disillusioned with the man who has championed him all his life, refuses to consider re-taking his exam and becomes a drifter.

Again one can sympathize with Biff after this traumatic experience, but one has to decide if it is enough to explain and excuse Biff's deterioration into a life of escape and self-pity, or whether it merely aggravates the consequences of an already weak will.

A further point in the defence of Biff is contained in his indictment of the complexities of modern civilization and their stultifying effect:

'. . . it's a measly manner of existence. To get on that subway on the hot mornings in summer. To devote your whole life to keeping stock, or making phone calls, or selling or buying. To suffer fifty weeks of the year for the sake of a two-week vacation, when all you really desire is to be outdoors, with your shirt off. And always to have to get ahead of the next fella.'

Miller strikes a chord in most of us in this scorn of the rat-race, and awakens our instinctive longing to return to nature in Biff's next words:

'This farm I work on, it's spring there now, see? And they've got about fifteen new colts. There's nothing more inspiring or – beautiful than the sight of a mare and a new colt.' We are reminded of the music which heralds the opening of the play and echoes through it: *A melody is heard, played upon a flute. It is small and fine, telling of grass and trees and the horizon.* And we are reminded of the changes civilization has wrought: 'The street is lined with cars. There's not a breath of fresh air in the neighbourhood. The grass don't grow any more ...' Is the modern environment partly to blame for Biff's failure to grow, too?

Biff has good qualities. A comparison with brother Happy often illuminates these. There is no doubt of his love, as an adolescent, for his father. On Willy's return from a selling trip, Biff exclaims, 'Where'd you go this time, Dad? Gee we were lonesome for you.' And then, 'Gee, I'd love to go with you sometime, Dad!' He says he won't be nervous at the ball-game if his father is there, and he is going to score a touch-down especially for him. He has many friends of his own age but, 'When Pop comes home they can wait.'

In the 'present time' of the play we find Biff obviously concerned about his father's health. He hears him talking to himself and asks, 'God Almighty, Mom, how long has he been doing this?' And, although he is disillusioned, he still means to help – he offers to stay in the city he hates and give half his pay cheque to his father.

In the restaurant scene he tries hard to make his brother take his father's condition seriously by producing the rolled-up gas hose from his pocket to prove that Willy was contemplating suicide. At the end of the play he tries desperately to break through his father's illusions and bring him to the truth about both of them: 'Pop, I'm nothing! I'm nothing, Pop. Can't you understand that? There's no spite in it any more. I'm just what I am, that's all.'

Unlike Happy, Biff seems, at the end of the play, to find himself. The truth hurts, but he is honest and brave enough to face it. After kidding himself that his first job with Oliver was as a salesman, and now failing completely to gain even an interview with him, he says:

'I even believed myself that I'd been a salesman for him! And then he gave me one look and – I realized what a ridiculous lie my whole life has been. We've been talking in a dream for fifteen years. I was a shipping clerk.'

When his father arrives he tries unsuccessfully to make him face the truth too: 'Let's hold on to the facts tonight, Pop. We're not going to get anywhere bullin' around. I was a shipping clerk'; and when he and Happy have deserted their distraught father 'babbling in a toilet', Biff is filled with self-loathing and tells his mother he is the 'scum of the earth'.

   In his final scene with his father, Biff is still trying to force him to recognize the truth: 'We never told the truth for ten minutes in this house!' he cries, '. . . Will you take that phony dream and burn it before something happens?' In vain, so far as Willy is concerned. But later, in the 'Requiem', to Happy, who is still dreaming his own dreams, Biff says, 'I know who I am, kid.' Unlike the others, he has discovered himself.

Happy

He, like his brother, is lost, but in a different way.

Unlike Biff, Happy has totally absorbed his father's indoctrination. He is thirty-two, and we are told he is:

. . . tall, powerfully made. Sexuality is like a visible colour on him, or a scent that many women have discovered. He, like his brother, is lost, but in a different way, for he has never allowed himself to turn his face toward defeat and is thus more confused and hard-skinned, although seemingly more content.

Happy continually boasts of his sexual prowess. 'About five hundred women would like to know what was said in this room,' he tells Biff in their shared bedroom. Yet in very occasional moments of truth he speaks of his frustrations: 'All I can do now is wait for the merchandise manager to die.' He goes on to describe how this manager built a very large estate and grew tired of it in two months and sold it, and he admits that he would be just as dissatisfied and restless. 'I don't know what the hell I'm working for ... But then, it's what I always wanted. My own apartment, a car, and plenty of women. And still, goddammit, I'm lonely.' A little later, he boasts that he can get gorgeous women whenever he likes: 'The only trouble is, it gets like bowling or something. I just keep knockin' them over and it doesn't meant anything.'

Physical assets outweigh all else – due, no doubt, mainly to Willy's indoctrination: 'I mean I can outbox, outrun, and outlift anybody in that store, and I have to take orders from those common, petty, sons-of-bitches till I can't stand it any more.' Happy blames the system for any moral weakness on his part: 'See, Biff, everybody around me is so false that I'm constantly lowering my ideals . . .'

For a time he is attracted to Biff's idea of living the open-air life together, and agrees with Biff that they were not brought up to grub for money. But, when Biff immediately says 'Then let's go!' Happy replies, 'The only thing is – what can you make out there?'

By comparison with Biff, Happy is an unsympathetic character. He boasts of ruining a girl who is engaged to be married in five weeks, and adds that it is the third time that this has happened. He admits to taking bribes, pretends he hates himself for it, but in reality is rather proud. Despite his thinking otherwise he is indifferent to his father's deteriorating health and insufficiently interested to have realized that his parents are in financial difficulty. His mother, upbraiding her sons for just this, calls him 'a philandering bum!'

Happy has, however, one claim on our sympathy: he is completely overshadowed by his elder brother. It is pathetic to see him trying to win some of his father's approval for himself; twice, as a child, we hear him attempt unsuccessfully to attract Willy's attention: 'I'm losing weight, you notice, Pop?', but Pop doesn't notice. And as an adult he vies for the limelight: 'I'm gonna get married, Mom' fails to arouse a flicker of interest.

In the restaurant scene, however, we see the truth of his mother's description of him. It is supposed to be a treat and celebration for his father, but he is only interested in chatting up a call-girl, impressing her with a series of lies. His brother, he says, is a big cattle man from the West and a quarter-back with the New York Giants; he himself was at West Point. He arranges for the girl to find a friend for Biff and, when Willy enters, he tries to dissuade Biff from confessing the truth – that he did not even reach an interview with Oliver.

When Willy, on the point of nervous collapse, makes for the wash-room, Biff tries to impress upon Happy the fact that their father is desperate by producing the piece of gas pipe – he then hurries from the restaurant, and Happy, following with the girls, denies his father: 'No, that's not my father. He's just a guy. Come on, we'll catch Biff, and, honey, we're going to paint this town!'

In the final show-down between Biff and his father, Biff tries to break through the illusion but Happy attempts to maintain it:

Biff We never told the truth for ten minutes in this house!
Happy We always told the truth!

And then Biff calls his brother's bluff: 'You big blow, are you the assistant buyer? You're one of the two assistants to the assistant, aren't you?' And Happy lamely replied, 'Well, I'm practically—.'

In the 'Requiem' Happy clings to the 'dream':

'All right, boy. I'm gonna show you and everybody else that Willy Loman did not die in vain. He had a good dream. It's the only dream you can have – to come out number-one man. He fought it out here, and this is where I'm gonna win it for him.'

The words are almost fine until one remembers that the 'good dream' led only to suicide and until one places the 'I'm gonna win it for him' in context against Happy's own self-delusion throughout the play.

The author's comment on Happy's last speech is surely contained in the stage direction that follows:

Biff (with a hopeless glance at Happy) . . .

Linda

You're my foundation and my support, Linda.

Linda is not quite so easy to understand as a first reading might suggest. We see at once that she is devoted to Willy and does all she can to try to calm the troubled waters he sails. She knows his life is based on an illusion, and she willingly lives the lie with him rather than hurt him by trying to make him face the truth. She delights in her sons only when they do not oppose her husband; when that happens we see a much tougher side of her nature.

The author says of her in his directions

. . . she more than loves him, she admires him, as though his mercurial nature, his temper, his massive dreams and little cruelties, served her only as sharp reminders of the turbulent longings within him, longings which she shares but lacks the temperament to utter and follow to their end.

We find her, at the beginning of Act 1, trying to ease Willy's anguish at the exhaustion which has led to his uncontrolled driving. She finds excuses: the steering mechanism, his glasses; and, counselling rest, she takes off his shoes for him and begs him to try for an office job with his firm in New York.

She is happy to see both her sons at home again, and tries to play the role of peacemaker by telling Willy he shouldn't have criticized Biff and must not lose his temper with him. '*With infinite patience*' she suffers his neurotic outbursts over trivialities such as the wrong cheese, and responds sanely and kindly to his swift changes of mood:

Willy You're my foundation and my support, Linda.
Linda Just try to relax, dear. You make mountains out of mole-hills.

Linda is not taken in by his exaggeration of his sales; his twelve hundred gross soon come down to two hundred gross under her questioning, but she does not decry the dream; she just calmly calculates their debts against their income.

When Willy suddenly descends into deep depression at his failure, she cheers him with such remarks as: 'But you're doing wonderful, dear.' Or: 'And the boys, Willy. Few men are idolized by their children the way you are.'

Obviously Linda is to be admired for her loyal, brave support of a failing husband, but one must consider the irony of the situation: her very attempts to 'paper over the cracks', to foster the dream, are themselves helping to bring about the catastrophe.

Linda has a further burden to bear – her sons' indifference to their father's plight. She is forthright in accusing them of this indifference and tells Biff: '. . . if you don't have any feeling for him, then you can't have any feeling for me . . . He's the dearest man in the world to me, and I won't have anyone making him feel unwanted and low and blue.'

Her anguished account of her husband's dilemma, spoken to her sons to try to induce some feelings in them, summarizes and emphasizes for the audience Willy's tragedy and her own pain. She knows the truth of his life behind the dream, and out of love for him she does nothing about the symptoms of approaching disaster. 'How can I insult him that way?' she asks. While sympathizing greatly with her, one should consider her inaction carefully.

The start of Act 2 sees her behaving brightly and optimistically, delighting in the fact that Willy has slept well, and that her boys are home. She foretells a new and happier future for the family: 'It's changing, Willy, I can feel it changing!' She exhorts Biff to be loving to his father 'Because he's only a little boat looking for a harbour.'

The mood changes completely when Happy and Biff return from what should have been a celebration with their father. We see Linda flaring with disgust. Furiously she knocks their proferred flowers to the floor and challenges Biff: 'Don't you care whether he lives or dies?' She lashes both of them with her tongue: 'Did you have to go to women tonight? You and your lousy rotten whores! ... You're a pair of animals!' Linda is so often on the defence in this play, so often representing sanity and kindliness, symbolizing the day-to-day security of trying to make ends meet, as opposed to the glamorous and dangerous doctrine of Uncle Ben the fortune-maker, that it comes as an impressive surprise when we see this spirited, attacking side of her nature.

The end of Act 2 brings to Linda the horror of a demented Willy trying to plant seeds by torchlight, and of her son confronting his father with his contemplated suicide.

She tries, as always, to protect Willy from Biff, and to get him to go to bed to prevent disaster; but the situation is beyond her. She hears the car starting and then moving away at full speed. She can only cry 'No!'

In the 'Requiem', by her expressions of surprise that no one but the family are at the funeral – 'Why didn't anybody come?' – Miller ironically reminds us of that other funeral, described by Willy to Howard: 'When he died, hundreds of salesmen and buyers were at his funeral.'

Linda, bewildered, cannot understand why Willy had to die when for the 'First time in thirty-five years we were just about free and clear. He only needed a little salary. He was even finished with the dentist.' And, in her final speech: 'Willy, dear, I can't cry. Why did you do it? ... And there'll be nobody home.'

Some find Linda's bewilderment – and her obsession with

materialistic matters – inconsistent. They feel that she must have had a more intimate knowledge of Willy's dilemma than simply to believe that he killed himself because he was in debt. They accuse Arthur Miller of allowing inconsistency in order to extract the last ounce of agony – as he certainly does – from these pathetically uncomprehending last words. But it must also be borne in mind that Linda is emotionally distraught, and that '*she ... lacks the temperament to follow to their end*' the longing in Willy's heart. Hers is a down-to-earth, simple nature, content just to be involved in everyday affairs.

Charley

You been jealous of me all your life, you damned fool!

'Uncle' Charley is an interesting contrast to Willy. He acts with reason, is usually unbiased, unemotional and always sure of himself. Charley has his own business and does not need to travel. Willy, condemning himself for talking too much, admits that Charley is a man of few words and is respected. Biff contrasts Charley with his own father, saying that Charley would never behave in the uncontrolled way his father has in his own house. No wonder there is more than a hint of jealousy in Willy's attitude to Charley, evidenced in his comment: 'He's liked, but he's not well liked.'

Miller's directions describe Charley as '... *a large man, slow of speech, laconic, immovable. In all he says, despite what he says, there is pity, and now trepidation.*' The pity and the trepidation are there on Charley's first appearance. He has, no doubt, heard some of Willy's outbursts of anguish through the thin walls and, worried, he has come to try to help. In his kindness, he suggests a game of cards to Willy to tire him a little, ready for sleep. He tries to humour him. He offers him a job with his own firm. But Willy reacts wildly, talking to an imaginary Ben, and finally quarrelling with Charley over the cards until Charley tells him he ought to be ashamed of himself, and leaves.

In Act 2, in a return to the past, he counters Willy's excessive emotional intensity over Biff's departure for the ball-game that afternoon with a little kindly banter. Later in the act the contrast to Willy is very clear, in the scene in Charley's office. He shows that he too is proud of his son, but in a different way. Bernard, now a lawyer, is to argue a case in the Supreme Court:

Willy The Supreme Court! And he didn't even mention it!
Charley He don't have to – he's gonna do it.
Willy And you never told him what to do, did you? You never took any interest in him.
Charley My salvation is that I never took any interest in anything.

Charley faces life in a practical, down-to-earth manner, but he is far from being a cold, money-making, business machine; witness his kindness shortly after the above extract. When Willy asks him for more than the fifty dollars Charley usually 'lends' him, Charley reminds him that there is always a job for him with his firm and, when Willy's pride rises and he refuses, Charley gives him the extra money he needs.

In the 'Requiem' Charley comforts Linda and answers her bewildered questioning with his wise comment: 'No man only needs a little salary.'

In his last speech he blames the merciless nature of the profession of salesman for the tragedy, and, although this is only partly responsible, it is a kindly statement of understanding and faith in his late friend Willy.

Bernard

A quiet, earnest, but self-assured young man.

Bernard, Charley's son, is a contrast to the two Loman brothers. Willy refers to him as an 'anacmic' and says that, although he gets the best marks in school, when the three boys go out in the world, the Loman brothers will be 'five times ahead' of Bernard because they have the popular personalities and the looks that Bernard lacks. This is another of Willy's dreams to be shattered before the end of the play.

On his first appearance, in the 'past time' of the play, Bernard is warning Biff, in front of his father, that he heard his tutor say he was going to fail Biff in his mathematics examination unless he worked. This precocious behaviour does not exactly endear him to us, even if he is right.

On his next appearance he again warns Willy that Biff will fail, and worse, certainly from a schoolboy's point of view, he announces that Biff is driving the car without a licence, and that his tutor thinks he is 'stuck up'.

On the morning of the ball game, Bernard behaves more in keeping with his age and competes with Happy to carry their hero, Biff's, gear so that he can get into the club-house. But later in the play he cannot conceal his excitement in announcing Biff's examination failure to Linda.

However, moving to the 'present time' of the play, we find that Bernard has grown into '*a quiet, earnest, but self-assured young man*'. He is now a successful lawyer, married, with two children.

Bernard greets Willy in his father's office when he is visiting there on his way to Washington to 'argue a case' in the Supreme Court. But he does not boast of this merely saying 'Oh, just a case I've got there, Willy'. It is Charley who later mentions the Supreme Court. Bernard cannot understand Biff's sudden loss of confidence, which seems to have dated from the time he visited Willy in Boston; but such probings into the past hurt Willy's conscience, and the interview ends. Bernard departs for Washington and we see him no more in the play.

Uncle Ben

... when I was seventeen, I walked into the jungle, and when I was twenty-one I walked out. And, by God, I was rich!

Ben Loman was Willy's elder brother, who died in Africa a few weeks before the 'present time' of the play. His appearances are therefore only in Willy's overwrought imagination and none of the other characters really sees Ben in 'present time'. Nevertheless, he is a very 'real' character. Arthur Miller describes him as '*... a stolid man, in his sixties, with a moustache and an authoritative air. He is utterly certain of his destiny, and there is an aura of far places about him.*' His entrances are accompanied by 'Ben's Music', which is described as 'idyllic'. This is a hint of Ben's purpose: he represents Willy's dream of success, a romantic vision of diamonds found in faraway places.

Ben left home when Willy was nearly four years old, to find their father in Alaska; but, according to Ben, his geography was poor and he ended up in Africa, where he made his fortune.

There is a slightly sinister aura about Uncle Ben, which Linda senses. Her fear for Biff in the mock fight he has with Ben, promoted by Willy to show Biff's prowess, illustrates this. Biff is tripped by Ben and pinned to the ground by the point of Ben's umbrella aimed at his eye. Ben advises Biff: 'Never fight fair with a stranger, boy.'

Ben is always in a hurry to change continents. He leaves for

Alaska, promising to visit again on his way back to Africa. He keeps his promise and reappears after Willy's interview with Howard Wagner. He boasts at having settled his business so quickly in Alaska – 'Doesn't take much time if you know what you're doing.' Finding Willy has just been sacked, he tempts him to go to Alaska and manage some timberland for him – the great outdoor life, part of Willy's dream. Linda mistrusts the adventure and encourages Willy to resist this flight from security. Ben leaves with the words: 'There's a new continent at your doorstep, William. You could walk out rich. Rich!'

Ben's next appearance is at the end of the play. Willy has finally broken and is sowing seeds by torchlight. Willy hints to Ben of his plan to kill himself so that Biff can have the life insurance money to launch himself into success. At first Ben finds objections to this, but then goes away for a while to consider it. When he reappears for the last time he is in favour of the suicide and encourages Willy by comparing it to going into the jungle to fetch a diamond out. Almost his last words are, 'A perfect proposition all round.'

We have considered Ben as a 'real' character, though he is strictly one-dimensional, and in the original production by Elia Kazan he was acted more as an automaton. So it is not difficult to see him also as just a part of Willy's mind: the dream of the unattainable; the frustration of not having seized the opportunity, earlier in life, of escaping the chains of a routine existence; and, finally, the two sides of Willy's tortured mind, the one considering suicide cowardly and ineffective, the other considering it as his triumphant redemption in his son's eyes and the assurance of his son's success in life.

General questions plus questions on related topics for coursework/examinations on other books you may have studied

1 It has been suggested that Willy Loman is too naive and superficial a character to be the hero of a tragedy. Give detailed reasons for agreeing or disagreeing with this criticism.

Suggested notes for essay answer:
These are suggestions only. Fill in detail from your own close examination of the text. Bear in mind:
(a) Willy's living of the lie he has established; (b) his inability to distinguish between illusion (or even delusion) and reality; (c) his lack of judgment; (d) his moral lapses (mistress, football). Look closely at the meanings of *pathetic* and *tragic* and list qualities which you think show that Willy is either one or the other of these. (*Quote* in support of what you say.) You might consider, for example, the intensity and vitality with which he lives his dream and set it against his exhaustion/tiredness as the price he has to pay. Look too at his self-deception, his inability to settle, his relationship/antagonism with regard to Biff, the clues there are (flashbacks for instance) to his coming breakdown, his admissions of failure (fat, garrulous), his relationships with Linda, then Charley (jealousy), Uncle Ben etc. Bring in his being sacked, borrowing money, the seed-sowing incident. Sum up by including his identity crisis (he never knew who he was) and weigh in the balance his living a false dream as against his trying to be successful and loved. *Quote* in support of what conclusion you come to.

2 'To me the tragedy of Willy Loman is that he gave his life, or sold it, in order to justify the waste of it.' (Miller) Discuss this statement fully.
3 How much do you blame the tragedy on Willy, and how much on his environment?
4 Miller admits that the play is 'slippery' to categorize, but he maintains strongly that it is a tragedy. Give your views on this.
5 What criticisms does the play level at the American way of life?
6 Trace Biff's development throughout the play. To what

extent is he a character with whom you can sympathize, or even identify?

7 Contrast the two brothers, Biff and Happy. How far do you consider they are victims of their father's indoctrination?

8 Assess the character of Linda. Do you find her always credible and always consistent?

9 What functions in the play are performed by Charley and Ben?

10 What have you found of interest in Miller's dramatic technique in this play?

11 Discuss Miller's use of any three of the following

(a) time changes, (b) scenery, (c) lighting, (d) music, (e) language.

12 'What I am working for is the gasp,' Miller said. 'I used to stand at the back of the theatre when "Death of a Salesman" was playing and hear it.' Do you find this a very moving play? Where in the play would Miller be likely to hear gasps from the audience?

13 Write about a book you are studying which deals with conflict between parents and children.

14 Say what part dreams, real or waking, play in a book or play you know well.

15 Write about a character who acts in an irresponsible way in your chosen book.

16 Examine the presentation of marriage in a book you know well, saying which partner, husband or wife, is to blame for anything that goes wrong.

17 Give an account of the importance of sport or music or of any specialist activity in a book you know well.

18 Compare any two characters who are friends or relations in your chosen book.

19 Describe the ending of any book or play you know which is sad, and say how the author gets an emotional or sympathetic response from audience or reader.

20 Write about any book you have read which deals with an aspect or aspects of American life.

Further reading

Other plays by Arthur Miller that are available in paperback editions include the following:

All My Sons (Heinemann Educational 1971)

Archbishop's Ceiling (Methuen Paperbacks 1984)

The Crucible (Penguin Modern Classics 1986)

Danger! Memory! (Methuen Paperbacks 1986)

Incident at Vichy (Penguin 1985)

Two-Way Mirror: 'Elegy for a Lady' and 'Some Kind of Love Story' (Methuen Paperbacks 1984)

View From The Bridge (Penguin Modern Classics 1986)